W9-AHI-273

CHIANG MAI

APA PUBLICATIONS

Part of the Langenscheidt Publishing Group

L

Welcome!

The ancient capital of northern Thailand is the starting point for a fascinating tour of antiquities, exotic hill tribes, and lush jungle-covered mountains. This is where the ancient Lanna culture of Northern Thailand flourished for centuries, evidenced by some of the most beautiful temples and art in Asia. Adding to Chiang Mai's charm are its amiable people, ever ready to lend a helping hand to visitors.

Insight Guides' Bangkok-based correspondent Steve Van Beek makes sense of this cultural hot-spot with his diverse itineraries. From full-day trips taking in the glittering temples of the city to shorter options that range the gamut from racuous markets to placid rafting trips, and week-long excursions to the mist-shrouded Mae Hong Son and the notorious Golden Triangle region, Van Beek has it all covered. Chapters on eating out, shopping and nightlife, and a useful practical information section complete the Chiang Mai experience.

 Steve Van Beek first visited Chiang Mai in the 1970s, fuelled by visions of a beautiful land trod by a genteel people. Crammed amongst returning Northerners in a third-class train bound for Chiang Mai from Bangkok, Van Beek had his first glimpse of the broad valley formed by the Chao Phraya River, and his first taste of Thai hospitality: by the time the train chugged into the rickety Chiang Mai station, he had at least a half-dozen invitations to spend the night. Van Beek has returned time and time again, to renew old acquaintances, and also to re-affirm his vision of this beautiful land.

C O N T E N T S

Pages 2/3:
hilltribe village
in Doi Thong,
Chiang Mai

Pages 8/9: hilltribe children at their colourful best

History of North Thailand

Lanna, land of a million rice fields, is the name by which the North and its culture has been known for centuries. Bordered by the Mekong River and the mountains of Burma, and walled off by jungle from the Central Plains, Lanna lived in remote splendour until early this century. The region had its own royal families, spoke its own dialect, and fought its own battles with Burmese and Siamese armies.

The early power bases were along the Mekong River. In the mid-13th century, King Mengrai marched south to create an empire in the Kok River Valley, establishing the city of Chiang Rai in 1262. After capturing Haripunchai (Lamphun) and securing joint leadership of Phayao, he sought a more central headquarters and looked for one in the Ping River Valley.

Here, Mengrai constructed a palace/fortress at Wiang Kung Kam (its remains are found just south of the Superhighway) and a temple, Chedi Liem, but as they were unsuitable he moved further north to establish Chiang Mai (New City) in 1296. Because the Ping River frequently overflowed its banks, Mengrai built his royal city on high ground to the west, surrounding it with a brick and earth wall 1½km (1 mile) on each side and surrounded by a defensive moat. A smaller wall, remnants of which can be found along Kamphaeng Din Road, once embraced a residential section.

The flowering of Lanna culture dates from the reign of warrior King Tilokaraja. So influential was he that the 8th World Buddhist Council was held in Chiang Mai in 1455. Less than a century later, however, the kingdom was embroiled in debilitating disputes, a situation the Burmese were quick to exploit. After repeated battles, Chiang Mai fell to King Bayinnaung of Pegu in 1558 and was ruled by the Burmese for the next two centuries.

While Burma spared Chiang Mai, the destruction that it visited upon Ayutthaya in 1767 was devastating. The Burmese conscripted Chiang Mai's young men and appropriated supplies for its war against Laos. So severe did the hardships become that, Chiang Mai, like other cities of the North such as Chiang Rai, Chiang Saen, Sukhothai and Phayao, were depopulated. Chiang Mai remained empty for 20 years until Prince Kawila triumphed over the Burmese in 1799 and established his headquarters in the city.

For most of the 19th century, Chiang Mai was ignored by Burma and Siam. It was not until the European colonial powers (the British in Burma and the French in Laos) began coveting the region that Bangkok's rulers realised their sovereignty over the area was in danger. In 1877, a Thai Viceroy took up residence in Chiang Mai and until 1939, ruled through a Chiang Mai prince.

The North acquired new importance with the dawn of the 20th century. A railway, begun in 1898, was pushed north through thick jungle and formidable mountains, the last rail being laid in 1921. The railway eliminated the torturous journey up the Chao Phraya and Ping rivers that took six weeks or more.

Prince Kawila, hero of Chiang Mai

The thickly-forested hills drew the attention of foreign teak merchants, who bought concessions and began floating logs down the rivers to Bangkok. When the concessions lapsed, the Forest Industry Organization took over and have since played a part in denuding much of the forested northern hills.

While cities to the south began to grow as a result of investment by the US government in support of the Indochina war, Chiang Mai remained stable. The last 15 years, however, have seen some dramatic changes. Farming is being modernised and in the southern valley, industrial plants are replacing rice seedlings. The city is experiencing rapid growth as condominiums and hotels mushroom high above the skyline. Once empty spaces are rapidly being filled with housing estates.

Yet, there are still pockets of the past in the back streets. And once the visitor steps outside the city, he discovers a different pace of life.

Northerners and the Hilltribes

Lanna Thais speak a dialect quite distinct from the people of the Central Plains. They are almost exclusively Theravada Buddhists although there are Mahayana Buddhists, Muslims and Sikhs in the larger towns. Of all the regions in Thailand where Christian missionaries strove to win converts, they were most successful in the

Rice seedlings

North, as the many churches attest. Missionaries also had considerable influence among the hilltribes, primarily the Lahus and the Karens.

Lanna Thais are largely lowland rice farmers, laboriously engineering the land into paddies in which they plant two crops of rice each year. Unlike Chinese villages which are inhabited by a single clan, Thai villages contain many unrelated families. Yet at planting and harvest time, they pool their labour for mutual benefit. The village is a democratic unit presided over by a *phu yai baan* (headman) or a *kamnan* (head of a group of villages) although he generally comes from the wealthiest family in the village. The Buddhist *wat* (temple) formerly anchored the village. Temple buildings served as meeting halls, the murals on the interior walls were illustrated instruction books on religion and the arts, and monks were the teachers, herbal doctors and arbitrators in village disputes. Although many of these functions have been taken over by government agencies, monks still continue to wield considerable influence.

In addition to the Thai peoples of Lanna, there are major racial groups like the Tai Yai and Tai Lu whose culture and languages

are similar. If theories are correct, most of these people originated in China and migrated south over 10 centuries ago. More recent arrivals include the Chinese and the hilltribes.

For most visitors, the hilltribes are the North's most colourful inhabitants. These tribal groups migrated from Himalayan foothills and southern China in the 19th century, moving across Burma and Laos to North Thailand. Although numbering approximately 550,000, or about one percent of the population, the Northern hilltribes are far from being a homogeneous group. Each of the six principal groupings – Hmong (Meo), Lisu, Akha, Lahu (Musur), Yao and Karen – have a distinct language incomprehensible to the others. Despite their differences, there is little conflict between them. No group claims a particular area as its own and villages intermingle and overlap throughout the North, especially along the borders with Burma.

These major tribal groupings are sub-divided according to the colours – Blue, White, or Red – of the costumes they wear. Each has its own patterns and styles of clothing. There are also lesser tribes like the elusive Phi Thong Luang (Spirits of the Yellow Leaves), Lua, H-tin, Kha-mu, and Wa.

As nomadic farmers, the hilltribes practise slash-and-burn agriculture by clearing a tract of forest and burning off the undergrowth to plant a crop. A few years later, when the soil's fertility has been

depleted by the crop, the hilltribe moves on to other virgin areas to begin the cultivation process all over.

Population pressures, a shortage of land, and government programmes to encourage the hilltribes to settle in particular areas, have reduced the peoples' nomadic instincts considerably. The government has also been successful in luring four of the tribes – Hmong, Yao, Akha, and Lisu – away from cultivation of opium. The crop has created a crime problem in the area known to the world as the Golden Triangle, where warlords operate illegal caravans and laboratories to process the poppy into heroin, in open defiance of the Thai government.

Projects initiated by His Majesty King Bhumibol in the 1970s provide seed and assistance to grow and market more

A typical hilltribe home

Lisu children who pose for photos may sometimes ask you for cash

socially acceptable crops. The northern hills have proven themselves to be as adaptable as the hilltribes, nourishing such diverse crops as asparagus, mushrooms, strawberries, apples and coffee.

The hilltribe culture, however, is proving fragile in the face of alien values introduced by the Thais and, in recent years, by the steady stream of tourists. The Thais have attempted to incorporate the hilltribes into the mainstream, more for chauvinistic reasons than in consideration for the needs of the latter. Needless to say, the toll has been heavy. Tourists were initially drawn by the unique cultures the tribes represented but their sheer numbers are threatening to overwhelm the tiny villages, creating an unhealthy dependence on outsiders.

The size, areas of habitation and characteristics of the six principal hilltribes are outlined below:

Karen: Numbering around 300,000, the Karens are the largest hilltribe in Thailand but are minor in comparison to the nearly five million in neighbouring Burma. They are thought to have originated in Tibet more than 2,600 years ago and have lived here for 200 years. Karens are concentrated west of Chiang Mai, northwest of Chiang Rai, and along the border to Phetchaburi.

Hmong (Meo): The best-known of the hilltribes, their 70,000 members live near the Laotian border, north and east of Chiang Mai. There are also a few Hmong villages south of Tak.

Yao: Their forefathers migrated from southern China about two centuries ago. While there are 1.3 million Yao in China and 200,000 in Vietnam, there are only 20,000 in Thailand, most of them around Chiang Rai, Nan, and near the Laotian border.

Lahu (Musur): Originating in Yunnan, China, the Lahu migrated into Thailand via eastern Burma in the last century. Now numbering 55,000, their villages are strewn along the Burmese border, north of Chiang Mai and near Chiang Rai.

Akha: Called 'dog eaters' because of their culinary preferences, the Akha originated south of Kunming in China's Yunnan province and began moving south about the turn of the century. They total 28,000 and live primarily north of Chiang Mai and Chiang Rai.

Lisu: Thought to have originated in eastern Tibet, Lisu are the latest arrivals, the first recorded tribesmen having settled here in 1921. Now numbering 24,000, they live near the Burmese border north of Chiang Mai and west of Chiang Rai.

Northern Culture

Although flavoured by contact with Burma and Laos, Lanna culture is unique. In addition to special dishes found only in the North, Lanna *wat* (temple) architecture is immediately recognizable.

Lanna-style temples are built on a low base of stucco-covered brick, and compared with the soaring temples of the Central Plains, a northern temple will seem rather squat. Typically, its roofs rise in three tiers from low, generally windowless, walls, sweeping in flat, graceful curves like the wings of a gigantic bird.

The bounty of northern teak forests has also allowed extensive use of wood both to clad the building and to provide deeply-carved decorations along its gable. The *viharn* (sermon hall) has a front portico supported by four columns. The upper sections of the spaces between the columns are curved like eyebrows, and are said to be a symbolic representation of hidden eyes watching over the populace.

The interior is generally plain. The most representative of Lanna

A typical Lanna temple Chiang Mai

structures is the kingpost construction to support the roof. The ceiling is also decorated with gold lotuses and stars on a red background. In newer temple buildings, there is a strong preference for gold and bright red colours, often to the point of garishness.

There are a number of *chedi* (stupa) styles including the square pyramid of the early Haripunchai period (Wat Kukut in Lamphun

15

A Yao woman

and Wat Chedi Liem in Chiang Mai), square pyramid with dented corners (Wat Chedi Luang and Wat Doi Suthep in Chiang Mai), the later Haripunchai style with its compact base and tall spire (Wat Phra That Haripunchai in Lamphun), and a circular chedi punctuated with niches holding standing Buddha images (Wat Rampoeng in Chiang Mai). Burmese temples with their half-dozen roofs, gingerbread eaves and distinctive Burmese-style *chedi* with golden rings like those of the 'long-necked' Karen (or Padaung) women are mainly found outside Lamphun and in Mae Hong Son.

The visitor to Chiang Mai has ample opportunity to study such monuments as there are scores scattered around the city. The temples are found everywhere: occupying vacant lots in villages, wedged between storefronts, and standing quietly behind bus stations, so ubiquitous that one soon begins to regard them as one does the trees dotting the landscape.

Another distinctive feature of Lanna architecture is found in the houses: Northern homes are generally built of teak with walls that slope outwards, not inwards like the houses of the Central Plains. Houses are said to represent the water buffalo on which the people are so dependent: the columns representing the beast's stout legs, the outward sloping walls and roof, the massive body, and the crossed peaks — called *galae* — the horns of the animals. Another feature of these Northern houses is the *haem yon* that is placed over the doorway and representing testicles in which the guardian power of the house resides.

In addition to the performing arts, Lanna artisans have refined decorative crafts to a high degree. Lacquerware, silversmithing, ceramics, wood carving and umbrella-making are among the many arts found in the North, especially in Chiang Mai.

Evening prayers at Doi Suthep

A Thai spirit house

Tribal arts are simpler but more colourful and primarily used to adorn the body. Silver is crafted into belts, necklaces, bangles and other jewellery. Coton fabrics are woven and embroidered with needlepoint or patchwork designs, most of which are derived from symbolic representations of nature and unique to the tribe that created them. Often, the embroidery created by a young girl is a means by which prospective in-laws determine her suitability as a wife.

Religion

Theravada Buddhism is the dominant religion, manifested by numerous temples and monks in their saffron robes. By tradition, a young man becomes a monk for a short time to better understand his religion; makes merit to atone for his sins so that when he's reincarnated, he will return as a higher being. Because women are not ordained, a monk also makes merit for his mother and sisters.

Each day at dawn, silent monks walk barefoot through the villages and towns to receive rice and curries from Buddhists who wait in front of their homes. On Wan Phra (four times a month) days, the faithful take food to the *wat* for the monks to eat after they have chanted ancient sermons in the Pali language. The three Buddhist holidays of Magha Puja, Visakha Puja, and Asalaha Puja are celebrated in all temples.

The North has many charming religious practices that recall the very human brand of Hinduism in Bali. At certain times of the year, you will find tiny hillocks of sand in a temple courtyard, each with a small flag waving from its summit. This practice is a clever way of obtaining earth to raise the temple compound above the floodwaters. Each person who carries a handful of sand to the temple makes merit. It does not take too many handfuls before the temple has all the sand it needs for its foundations or for the construction of new buildings. Every Buddhist temple will have a bodhi tree, symbolic of the tree under which the Buddha attained Enlightenment. To prolong the lives of the ancient bodhi tree, whose leaves end in a distinctive, claw-like point, villagers bring poles to prop up its tired old limbs, giving the branches much-needed support and earning merit for themselves in the process.

Still, as Thai Buddhists like to make sure they cover all the bases, they practice a form of animism alongside their belief in Buddhism. Nearly every home has a small shrine where the spirits reside. To these, the Thais offer incense and flowers to ensure protection in their daily lives. The North is also home to a significant number of Chinese, who worship Taoist deities in Chinese temples. There is also a small Thai and foreign Christian community and there are Islamic mosques throughout the city.

The hilltribes are mostly animist, believing in spirits that protect the village and which must not be offended. The list of possible transgressions is lengthy. Some, like the Akha, build spirit gates which protect the village from malevolent ghosts. If one touches it or the column of a Karen house, one must donate a pig for sacrifice.

Thai Values

While Buddhism is the prime influence shaping Thai moral behaviour there are several other important values. One is *sanuk*, a concept which translates roughly as 'fun'. Thais judge the value of an endeavour by the amount of *sanuk* it has; anything not *sanuk* is to be avoided. Another Thai attitude worth understanding is that of *mai pen rai*, which is related to the Buddhist ideal of avoiding suffering. *Mai pen rai* is translated variously as 'it doesn't matter' or 'no problem', and is usually accompanied by a shrug of the shoulders.

The surprise is that despite this attitude, the Thais are a dynamic people as the rapid development of the country amply demonstrates.

The Thais are an immensely practical people

Historical Highlights

3,500 BC: Bronze Age culture flourishes at Ban Chieng in Thailand's northeast.

8th–13th century: Chinese migrants arrive in north Thailand.

1238: Khmer power wanes and Thais establish an independent nation based at Sukhothai.

1262, 1296: Mengrai establishes Chiang Rai and Chiang Mai.

1350: Farther south on the Chao Phraya River, a new power emerges at Ayutthaya that supplants Sukhothai's dominance.

1451 and 1508: Chiang Mai wars with Ayutthaya.

1545: A powerful earthquake destroys parts of Chiang Mai, including the upper portion of Wat Chedi Luang.

1558: Chiang Mai is defeated and occupied intermittently for two centuries by Burma.

1598: Ayutthaya defeats and occupies Chiang Mai but subsequently loses it to Burma.

1767: After repeated attempts, Burmese armies raze Ayutthaya. The Thai army regroups at Thonburi and for 15 years wars with the Burmese, Laotians and Vietnamese.

1774: Chiang Mai is abandoned.

1782: The wars subside. General Chakri assumes the throne. Taking the name of Rama I, he moves his capital to Bangkok.

1796: Prince Kawila re-populates Chiang Mai.

1809: Bangkok's major buildings are completed, Rama II re-creates the literature and arts that were destroyed at Ayutthaya.

1851: King Mongkut ascends the throne and sets Thailand on the path towards modernisation.

1868–1910: King Chulalongkorn continues his father's initiatives, moves Siam into the 20th century. He also preserves its sovereignty, making it the only Southeast Asian nation to escape colonisation.

1874: Bangkok decides to administer Chiang Mai through a royal commissioner.

1910–1925: King Vajiravudh concentrates on political reforms, giving greater freedom to his people, and encouraging criticism of government policies.

1921: The railway from Bangkok to Chiang Mai is completed.

1932: A revolution in Bangkok replaces absolute monarchy with a constitutional monarchy.

1939: Chiang Mai becomes a province and is ruled directly from Bangkok.

1941–1945: In World War II, Thailand is occupied by the Japanese.

1950–1972: On May 5 1950, Bhumibol is officially crowned as king. A succession of coups and military-backed governments follow soon after. In the 1960s, Thailand experiences an economic boom as a result of investment by the US in support of the Vietnam war.

1973–90: A popular uprising topples a despised dictatorship, ushering in a three-year period of democracy. However, a right-wing counter-coup in 1976 re-establishes military rule. Several governments are chosen in popular elections, but always with the military in the background.

1991: Public reaction over a military coup against a supposedly corrupt government results in the appointment of Anand Panyarachun as Prime Minister.

1992: In May, public demand for a return to democracy leads to an army massacre that leaves hundreds dead. In September, elections are held and a new government under Prime Minister Chuan Leekpai is formed.

1995: In July, the leading opposition party Chart Thai is elected to power, with Barnharn Silpaarcha nominated as Prime Minister. In December the same year, the 18th Southeast Asian Games are held in Chiang Mai.

1996: Chiang Mai celebrates its founding 700 years ago.

1997:: In July a serious recession hits Thailand and much of the rest of Southeast Asia. By the end of the year a new government is formed, again under the leadership of Chuan Leekpai.

North Thailand

40 km / 25 miles

Mae Sai

Doi Tung

Chiang Saen

The Golden Triangle

Menam Khong

Chiang Khong

Ban Houay Sai

Tha Charoen

Muang Houn

Mae Salong

Mae Chan

Nam Mae Kok

1837

Muang Pakbeng

Wiang Chai

Chiang Rai

L A O S

Sop Huai

Nam Mae Ing

Thoeng

Mekong

Mae Suai

Phan

Pa Daet

Chiang Kham

Pan

Huai Kon

2153

Wiang Pa Pao

1854

Chun

Song Khwae

Chiang Klang

Na Pu

Mae Chai

Ban Dong

Pong

Ban Pua

2121

Bo Luang

Mae Khachan

Phayao Kwan

Phayao

Mae Nam Nan

Tha Wang Pha

Wang Nua

Mae Nam Wang

Sila Phet

T H A I L A N D

Pa Poel

Nan

Ban Tong

Pan Nua

Nam Poon

Hok

Chae Hom Reservoir

Ngao

Mae Charim

Mae Nam Yom

Pha Tai Caves

Wiang Sa

Mae Nam Wa

Kiu Lom Reservoir

Pang La

Ban Pa Daeng

Uam

Thung Nao

Na Noi

Sali

Ban Phae

Rong Kwang

Lampang

Phrae

Muang Pak-Lay

Wiang Ko Sai

Phan Soeng

Long

Sung Men

Doi Phaya Fo

1465

Ban Khok

Wang Chin

Den Chai

Sirikit Reservoir

Phu Yen

1032

Chong Na Siam

Mayom

Phu Soai Doao

2102

Muang Kenthao

Mae Hu

Uttaradit

Ban Pak Pat

Nam Pat

Mae Nam Nan

Heung Huang

Tha Li

Day Itineraries

Although Thai Airways offers several daily flights – each taking 60 minutes – to Chiang Mai, it is more fun to travel by train. The day train from Bangkok to Chiang Mai covers 697km (433 miles) in 13 hours (see the *Practical Information* chapter for details), but during the winter and the monsoon seasons, the arduous ride is compensated for by wonderful views of green trees and lush rice fields as far as the eye can see. In the hot season (late February through May) though, the fields are parched and unattractive, so you may want to consider flying instead. If views are not your top priority, consider taking the overnight air-conditioned sleeper train (there are several departures daily) which arrives in Chiang Mai in the morning, saving you money on a night's hotel accommodation and enough daylight to take in some of the sights of Chiang Mai.

The 'Rose of the North' has not escaped the modernisation that is enveloping the whole of Thailand. Trees have been replaced with street lamps, concrete shophouses for teak houses and noisy *tuks tuks* for the silent and rapidly-disappearing *samlors* (pedal trishaws). And yes, there are traffic jams even this far north. Still, the concrete and cacophony cannot mask the captivating charm of Chiang Mai.

Departing from Bangkok's Hualampong Station

The *Day Itineraries* in this book sufficiently cover all the must-see sights of Chiang Mai, including the magnificent Wat Phra That Doi Suthep, in two full days. The *Pick & Mix* and *Excursions* sections are for visitors with the time and inclination to explore the cool air of the mountains, hilltribe villages, elephant camps and other delights of the northern hills.

Note: In the itineraries that follow, 'H' refers to the Highway number and 'KM' to the kilometre post numbers that you will see by the side of the road.

Chiang Mai City Tour

A day to savour the flavour and layout of Chiang Mai. Spend the day exploring the area between the city wall and the river.

If you haven't just stepped off a plane or the overnight train, or had breakfast at your hotel, make **Tha America** your first stop. Located at 402 Tha Phae Road, it opens at 7.30am and, as its name suggests, serves good American-style breakfasts and excellent coffee plus a selection of snacks. Keep it light as you will have an early lunch today.

After breakfast, exit left and walk 200m (230yds) to the first of four temples you will visit along Tha Phae Road. Wat Chetawan, Wat Mahawan, Wat Boopharam and Wat Saen Fang are not the most stunning of Chiang Mai's temples but they do give a good introduction to the dominant architectural styles of the North. **Wat Chetawan**, with its three Burmese-style *chedi*, is undergoing extensive reconstruction. It may be several years before the *viharn* (sermon hall) is ready for its superb woodcarved gable to be restored to where it belongs.

Cross Tha Phae Road to **Wat Mahawan**. Perched on its wall are Burmese-style figures which guard a Burmese-style *chedi* and *viharn*. Compare the *viharn* with the Lanna-style *bot* (ordination hall), marked by six boundary stones, or *bai sema*, around it. On the same side of the street, about 150m (165yds) to the east (against the traffic) is

Wat Chetawan spire

23

↗ Chang Kien Falls

Chiang Mai Hospital, Lanna Golf Course ↗

↗ Mae Rim, Mae Taeng, Chiang Dao, Fang, Mae Ai

Lanna Hos...

Thai German Dairy, Doi Pui, Arboretum Zoo, Huai Kaeo Falls, Doi Suthep, Phuping Palace,

Babylon

Chiang Mai National Museum

Chotana Rd.

Chiang Mai Phucome

Wat Jet Yot

Wa... Ta...

Chiang Mai University

Huai Kaeo Rd.

Chorprathan Rd. (Canal Rd.)

Chang Pheuak Bus Station ▶

White Eleph... Statue

The Pub

Chiang Pheuak Rd.

Wat Chiang Yuen

Amari Rincome

Tribal Research Centre

Hasadsewi Rd.

Chiang Mai Orchid

Manee Nopparat Rd.

Chang Pheuak Gate

Wat Chiang...

Foot of the Mountain

Suan Sukaphap Sri Nakarin Fitness Park

Nimmanhaemin Rd.

Sri Mangalachan Rd.

Sri Tokyo

Boon Ruangrit Rd.

Arug Rd.

Sri Phum Rd.

Thai Airways Office

Singharat Rd.

Wiang Kaeo Rd.

Phrapokklao Rd.

Jail

Ratchawithi Rd.

Old Provincial Office

Wat Chi...

Wat D... Di...

Maharaj (Suan Dok) Hospital

Suthep Rd.

Suan Dok Gate

Wat Phra Singh

Ratchdamnoen Rd.

Chiang Come

Wat Pan Tao

Wat U-Mong

Wat Suan Dok

Sam Lan Rd.

Batchamanka Rd.

Wat Chedi Luang

Phra Pokklao Rd.

Top G.H...

1 Alliance Francaise
2 Anusarn Market
3 Chumpol Guesthouse
4 D.K. Books
5 Diamond
6 Galare Guesthouse
7 Governor's Residence
8 Honey Chicken Restaurant
9 Mae Ping Post Office
10 Wat Lamchang
11 Montri
12 Pornping
13 Riverside Restaurant
14 Sangtawan Cinema
15 Sompet Market
16 Statue of the Three Kings
17 Suriwong Book Centre
18 The Gallery Restaurant
19 Ton Lamyai Market
20 U.S.I.S.
21 Wat Chai Sri Phum
22 Wat Chetawan
23 Wat Saen Fang
24 Whole Earth Restaurant

Buak Hat Park

Suan Prung Gate

Bumrung Buri Rd.

Chang Loh Rd.

Chiang Mai Gate

Batchiangsa...

Silversmith

Aom Muang Rd.

Thipanet Rd.

Wua Lai Rd.

Wualai Rd.

Suriwong Rd.

Lanna Folk Museum

Immigration Office

Chiang Mai Airport - International & Domestic

Banyen

Day 1

Itinerary 2

Itinerary 3

↙ Hang Dong, San Pa Tong, Chom Thong, Hot, Mae Sariang

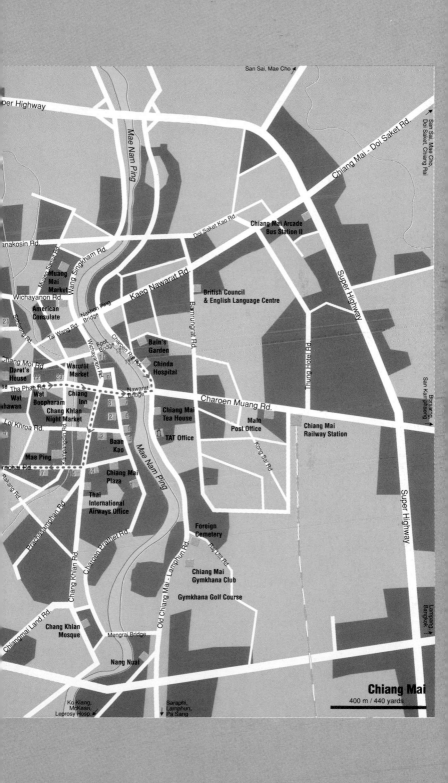

San Sai, Mae Cho ◄

ber Highway

San Sai, Mae Cho
Doi Saket, Chiang Rai ►

Chiang Mai - Doi Saket Rd.

Mae Nam Ping

Doi Saket Kao Rd.

Chiang Mai Arcade
Bus Station II

anakosin Rd.

Wang Singkham Rd.

Kaeo Nawarat Rd.

British Council
& English Language Centre

Muang
Mai
Market

Wichayanon Rd.

American
Consulate

Nawarat Ping
Bridge

Tai Wang Rd.

Foot
Bridge

Chiang Mai Rd.

Darat's
House

Tha Phae Rd.

Wat
Bahawan

Wat
Boopharam

Wichayanon Rd.

Warurōt
Market

Chiang
Inn

Charoen Rd. Soi

Bain's
Garden

Chinda
Hospital

Nawarat
Bridge

Charoen Muang Rd.

Chang Khlan
Night Market

Loi Khroa Rd.

Chiang Mai
Tea House

Chiang Mai
Railway Station

Main
Post Office

Bamrungrat Rd.

Thung Hotel Rd.

Super Highway

Kong Sai Rd.

TAT Office

Baan
Kao

Mae Nam Ping

Mae Ping

rechat Rd.

Kampaengdin Rd.

Chiang Mai
Plaza

Thai
International
Airways Office

Charoen Prathet Rd.

Foreign
Cemetery

Chiang Mai
Gymkhana Club

Gymkhana Golf Course

Chang Khlan Rd.

Old Chiang Mai - Lamphun Rd.

Praehasamohan Rd.

Hai Uli Rd.

Super Highway

San Kamphaeng

Lampang,
Bangkok ►

Chiangmai Land Rd.

Chang Khlan
Mosque

Mengrai Bridge

Nang Nual

Ko Klang,
McKean,
Leprosy Hosp. ►

Saraphi,
Lamphun,
Pa Sang

Chiang Mai

400 m / 440 yards

Wat Boopharam. Its new *viharn* is an odd mixture of styles, not at all harmonious. Under the Lanna-style roof is a square tower atop a blocky structure that is all filigree and frippery. The building holds what the abbot claims is the world's largest teak Buddha. The temple's prize building is the small wooden *viharn* to the right. Stucco decorations have been skillfully laid atop wood and topped with a Lanna-style roof.

The interior holds a large and a small gilded Buddha image. Once inside, you are transported to another world bearing little reference to the traffic rushing by outside.

Nearby are a number of small cafés where you may pause for a drink or snack before continuing on to **Wat Saen Fang** whose entrance gate looks like a separate temple in itself. Follow the undulating *naga* (mythical serpent) balustrade to the inner courtyard that holds a tall Burmese-style *chedi* defended by stucco *singha* (mythical lions) that stand guard along with several antique cannons. Beneath the windows of the Lanna-Burmese *viharn* are handsome panels depicting more mythical beasts. Decorating the eastern gables are fine carvings. To the west, along the roofline of the new *bot* are some lovely praying disciples.

Back on Tha Phae Road turn left and after about 300m (330yds) turn right on to Chang Khlan Road (Creeping Elephant Road). This road not only accommodates the celebrated **Night Market** (to which you will return on an evening trip later) but also a host of restaurants and three large hotels. Pause for lunch and to give your legs a rest. After lunch, continue your walk along Chang Khlan Road until you reach the traffic junction at a crossroad. Cross over to the Caltex petrol station and hail a *tuk-tuk* (three-wheeled motorised trishaw). Ask to be taken to **Banyen Silver Shop** at 86/1–3 Wua Lai Road.

Chiang Mai was once a collection of villages, many of which were devoted to the production of a particular craft. **Wua Lai** was once a silversmiths' village. Although most of the shops have moved to the San Kamphaeng Road area, the back streets of Wua Lai still resound with the tap-tapping of hammers in artisans' workshops. The Banyen Silver Shop has a rather small collection of modern and antique jewellery but it is the starting point for a wander through the side *soi* (lane).

Walk down the lane marked Wua Lai Soi 2. Along it you will find a number of silverworking studios. At No 28, you can watch the artisans at work under the house and then buy superbly crafted silver bowls in the living room at prices lower than those in shops. Alternatively, walk to Wua Lai Soi 3 to the **Siam Silverware Factory** (signs point the way to House No 5) which offers a wide selection of handicraft items.

Left, Wat Boopharam

Lanna Folk Museum occupies a traditional Northern Thai house

From Wua Lai Road, hail a *samlor* (pedal trishaw) for the 1-km (½-mile) ride to the **Lanna Folk Museum** on the left. In a lovely garden, the 130-year-old Lanna-style **Galae House** (open daily except Thursday 10am–4pm), which formerly sat on the banks of the Ping River, serves as an ethnological museum, providing a glimpse of life in a former age. Climb up the steps of Galae House and look at the antique household utensils, farm equipment and lovely lacquerware items on display.

Continue south on Wua Lai and cross the Superhighway intersection. The **Banyen** (open daily 8.30am–4.30pm, tel: 274007) sits on the far left-hand corner opposite the Airport Plaza Shopping Centre. In 1990, a fire destroyed the original premises on Wua Lai Road, but fortunately, the owner, Mrs Banyen, had already begun moving items to her new shop. Banyen's primary appeal is that it makes shopping fun.

The proud owner of the Banyen

Statues lie under trees and lean against old wooden houses, cluttering every corner so that when you least expect it, you stumble across a treasure. If nothing more, it is a pleasure to wander through the shop's compound. Artisans work while sleepy cats curl up on convenient statues and there is a wonderful air of informality about the entire yard at The Banyen. These are not antiques but very credible copies sold as home decor items.

A Banyen woodcraft

After freshening up at your hotel, have dinner overlooking the Ping River at **Riverside Restaurant** on Charoen Rat Road. The restaurant and the bar with live music attracts a lively crowd on most nights. After dinner, exit the restaurant to the right and cross **Nawarat Bridge**. Walk one block and turn left into the heart of the famous **Chang Khlan Night Market**. Here, scores of sidewalk vendors sell a superb array of goods, including tribal handicrafts, at very attractive prices. A word of warning: because of the throng of vendors and shoppers, keep a tight grip on your wallet or shoulder bag all the time.

DAY ②

Borsang and Doi Suthep

A visit to Borsang's handicraft studios and Chiang Mai's tallest hill with the stunning Wat Prathat Doi Suthep, Phuping Palace and a Hmong village. Evening at Chang Khlan Night Market.

Breakfast at your hotel or on the banks of the Ping at River View Lodge at the end of Soi 2, Charoen Prathet Road. Then catch a bus or drive to **Borsang Village**, travelling the 15-km (91-mile) stretch of road between Chiang Mai and the San Kamphaeng district. Red and white bus No 2259 leaves from Chang Pheuak Bus Station, travelling east along Charoen Muang Road. Alternatively, consider hiring a *samlor* for the entire morning for about 200 baht.

This morning is devoted to watching how Chiang Mai's ancient crafts are created, and then shopping for bargains. The eight shops listed here lie along the road to Borsang and have working studios that welcome visitors. A visit to all eight could easily turn a morning into a full day so you might want to pick and choose the crafts that interest you. Start just past the Superhighway intersection.

Napa Lacquerware, 8/2 San Kamphaeng Road (KM5.2), tel: 243039. Chiang Mai residents will argue that the fame of Burmese lacquerware is undeserved;

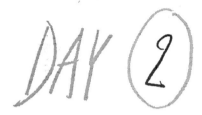

Ornate lacquer trays

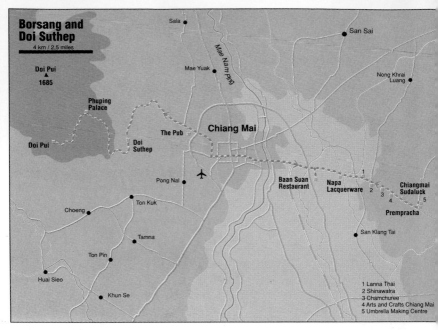

Borsang and Doi Suthep

4 km / 2.5 miles

Doi Pui
1685

Sala

San Sai

Mae Yuak

Nong Khrai Luang

Phuping Palace

Doi Pui

The Pub

Chiang Mai

Doi Suthep

Pong Nai

Baan Suan Restaurant

Napa Lacquerware

Chiangmai Sudaluck

Choeng

Ton Kuk

Prempracha

Tamna

San Klang Tai

Ton Pin

Huai Sieo

Khun Se

1 Lanna Thai
2 Shinawatra
3 Chamchuree
4 Arts and Crafts Chiang Mai
5 Umbrella Making Centre

that the Burmese artisans were in fact Thais who were enslaved by the Burmese and forced to work in their studios. Nonetheless, Chiang Mai seems to have retained enough artisans of its own to produce some fine work. Lacquerware comes in two varieties: gold leaf on glossy black, and green and black designs on a dark red base. Once found only in royal households, the principal items – betel boxes, servings trays, jewellery boxes – are produced in intriguing shapes created from bamboo and overlaid with lacquer. The studio also produces trays and containers covered in dyed eggshell crushed to create lovely mosaic designs.

Lanna Thai, 79 San Kamphaeng Road (KM6.1), tel: 338015/17. Silverware is another old Chiang Mai art. In addition to antique designs, the shop also produces hilltribe jewellery whose appeal lies less in its silver content (which is low) than in its artistry.

Shinawatra, 145/1-2 San Kamphaeng Road (KM7.1), tel: 338053/058. No craft is more representative of Thailand than Thai silk. Although generally associated with the Northeast, silk has found a home in Chiang Mai's many workshops. Observe how the silkworms are raised on a diet of mulberry leaves, their cocoons boiled in water and the filaments unwound and woven on hand looms into lengths of shimmering cloth.

Chamchuree Lapidary, 166/1 San Kamphaeng Road (KM7.5), tel: 338631. Burmese jade is imported in large quantities into northern Thailand where it is carved into pendants, earrings, bracelets and other pieces of jewellery.

Arts & Crafts Chiang Mai, 172 San Kamphaeng Road (KM7.8), tel: 338025.

A violet silk blouse set off by a gold brooch

Bronze-crafting is more prevalent in the Central Plains but the subjects are the same: Buddha images. Just look at some of the images in the Lanna temples, there you will find some the finest examples of bronze crafting in Thailand. Retail items range from religious to decorative.

Chiangmai Sudaluck, 99/9 San Kamphaeng Road (KM8.2), tel: 338006. With the Northern hills once abundantly covered in teak forests, it was natural that Chiang Mai would produce wood carvings.

Skilled woodwork is apparent in every northern temple; wood carving is a tradition carried on in this shop's studios. The shop specialises in furniture and home decor items.

Umbrella Making Centre, 111/2 San Kamphaeng Road (KM9), tel: 338324. Borsang, was once a tiny village where artisans laboured under their houses to craft bamboo, string and *sah* paper (made from the bark of the mulberry tree) into umbrellas that are a marvel of engineering. These were then painted with motifs from nature. The craft has since become an industry with a resultant loss of quality but the umbrellas are still produced by hand. A half-hour in an umbrella-making workshop is time well spent. This one, at the

Applying sah paper onto the bamboo ribs of an umbrella

intersection with the road to Doi Saket, is the best known.

Prempracha's Collection, on San Kamphaeng Road (KM9), tel: 338540. Ceramics are another well-known northern art, the most representative being celadon, a handsome light green glaze applied to lampstands, bowls and other items. Blue and white porcelain,

Phuping Palace, summer residence of the Royal Family

earthenware and *bencharong* (five-colour pottery) are also produced For lunch, return to KM4 and turn left to **Baan Suan** for delicious Thai food in a lovely garden setting 200m (230yds) away.

The afternoon and early evening is spent on **Doi Suthep**, the holy hill west of Chiang Mai. You may find it more convenient to rent a car for the afternoon as *tuk-tuks* are not allowed on the hill. If you prefer local transport, a mini-bus leaves from Tha Phae Road in front of the Bangkok Bank 100m (110yds) past the intersection with Chang Khlan Road) every 10 minutes for Doi Suthep, Phuping Palace and Doi Pui.

The steep road begins at the end of Huai Kaeo Road past the zoo, winding for 12km (7½ miles) up the flanks of Doi Suthep ('doi' is mountain) before reaching a parking lot. For the moment, forget about Wat Pra That Doi Suthep at the top of the hill. Instead, drive past the temple staircase and onto the road on the left which climbs through pine forests to **Phuping Palace**, 4km (2½ miles) farther on. Phuping is a summer residence used by the Royal Family as a headquarters for overseeing development projects in northern Thai and hilltribe villages. When the Royal Family is not in residence, the beautiful flower gardens are open to the public from 8.30am to 4pm Friday to Sunday and on official holidays. The gardens are well worth a visit.

Continue 3km (1¾ miles) to the Hmong village of **Doi Pui**. A visit here should give you some idea of hilltribe life. Unfortunately, the village has adapted a little too well to the tourist trade. Be ready for persistent offers to buy items or give money. If you would like to take a closer look at tribal beliefs and customs, there are several hilltribe treks you can go on (see *Excursion 12*).

Especially interesting in the village are the **Opium Museum** and the **Hilltribe Museum**. For centuries, the Hmong have been opium growers. The Opium Museum documents how the crop is cultivated and processed, and displays some of the implements used in opium production. In the Hilltribe Museum, the implements used in Hmong daily life are exhibited. These are of historical significance as many of the items displayed have been replaced by more modern ones and are no longer used.

Right, the Doi Pui countryside

At about 4pm, return along the road to **Wat Phra That Doi Suthep** (get your camera ready for superb views of it along the road), Chiang Mai's most famous temple. Perched high on the flank of the hill, 1,022m (3,000ft) above sea level, the temple has stood watch over Chiang Mai's dramatic changes over the past thirty years. Aside from minor alterations, the *wat* has remained what it always was: a peaceful retreat that lends itself to contemplation (except for days when it is overrun by tourists).

No visit to Chiang Mai – even for those who have visited it a dozen times – is complete without a long drive up the hill to the base of its *naga* (serpent) staircase. Although a funicular railway now glides to the top, resist the urge to take it. Instead, accumulate a bit of merit for yourself by climbing the 210 steps (304 if you count from the parking lot) to the summit. You will enjoy both a sense of relief and accomplishment when you reach the top. According to legend, the temple's site was selected by an auspicious elephant.

The story goes that a monk named Sumana placed half of a Buddha relic on an elephant's back and set it loose. It was decided that when the elephant stopped walking, a temple would be built on that exact spot to house the gem. The elephant must have had a perverse streak because instead of stopping at an easy site, it began climbing the hill. One can imagine the curses of the people trying to keep up with the pachyderm as it crashed through heavy jungle. The elephant seemed bent on walking to Burma but finally, to everyone's relief, it paused on the brow of the hill, trumpeted, turned around three times like a dog bedding down for the night, and lay down. That was the spot where Wat Phra That Doi Suthep was built.

Doi Suthep from afar

Take off your shoes and climb to the inner sanctuary of the temple. Anyone wearing shorts is barred from entering but they can rent sarongs near the entrance. Inside is a four-sided gilded brass

Doi Suthep, main courtyard

chedi which, like Bangkok's Wat Arun, seems to symbolise the North. Keep an eye out for the small *hong,* or mythical swan, on the length of wire stretching from the pinnacle to the base of the *chedi.* Thai Buddhists bestow their own blessings on the *chedi* by pouring water into the cup which the swan holds in its beak. The worshippers then turn the wheel on a pulley, raising the swan to the crown of the *chedi* where a small projection tips the cup, spilling the water down the sides of this sacred monument.

The complex abounds in odd memorials to chickens and other beasts. The *viharn* at either end hold several Buddha images, none of which has any real merit, and the murals in the cloisters have been ruined by repeated restoration. At 5pm monks gather in the western *viharn* for their evening prayers. Listen to their ethereal murmurings then exit the inner grounds. Ring the bells for good luck and walk to the balustrade to watch dusk gradually descend on Chiang Mai far below.

For dinner, you have a choice of either English or Thai-Chinese cuisine. For the former, drive down the hill to **Huai Kaeo Road**. On the right, 150m (164yds) before the intersection with the Super-highway, is **The Pub** serving typically English meals in a cosy dining room. In the winter, a fire blazes in the foyer for pre-prandial drinks. For delicious Thai-Chinese cuisine, go to **Khrua Sabai** at the golf-driving range, which is opposite the Airport Plaza.

After dinner, you may feel like visiting the **Chang Khlan Night Market** to shop. If not, ask at your hotel or guest house if there are any temple ceremonies being held that are worth watching.

These occasionally take place on certain full moon nights. During the full moon in October or November, there is the added attraction of the Loy Krathong festival.

Doi Suthep at Dawn

Now that you've seen Wat Phra Doi Suthep at dusk, return at dawn on another day for a contrasting view. To watch the sunrise over Chiang Mai from Doi Suthep with its chanting nuns and singing jungle birds, leave at about 5am for the expected sunrise at 6.30am. At this hour, there are few taxis so you will need a motorcycle or car. As it will be too early for vendors and most tourists, you have the place virtually to yourself. Nuns chant *sutras* in the *viharn* and jungle birds sing, creating a mystical atmosphere that is everything the exotic East represents. Walk to the parapet to watch the sky lighten and the sun rise over Chiang Mai.

PICK & MIX

1. Morning Market Walk

Rise at dawn for an early morning market tour. Choose from Ton Lamyai, Warorot and Muang Mai markets.

You have to rise early for this one because the market goes into full swing long before the sun comes up. Catch a *tuk-tuk* to Chiang Mai's oldest wet market, **Ton Lamyai**, at the end of Chang Moi Road next to the river. At one of the stalls, order a glass of Thai coffee, a potent brew of ground coffee and chicory. To go with it, ask for some *patongkoh*, a delicious deep-fried pastry that the Chinese eat for breakfast. Then begin exploring Ton Lamyai.

Thai wet markets are the equivalent of Western supermarkets, less hygienic but more atmospheric. Here, Thai housewives find everything they need to cook the day's meal. Fruits, vegetables and flowers, spices and herbs, and freshly-butchered meat and poultry are transported from the countryside of Chiang Mai to the markets, eventually ending up at the kitchens and dining tables of homes and restaurants. It is a great place to exercise your sense of smell and to gain a new and colourful dimension on life in Asia. Wander

Ton Lamyai market

around to see the wide variety of tropical produce on display. Across the street to the west is **Warorot market**, a warren of alleys where household goods, clothing, fabrics and hilltribe handicrafts are sold. Have a wander around even if you don't plan to buy anything.

On another morning, you might want to explore the **Muang Mai market**, just up the river past the Nakhon Ping Bridge. It is bigger and more modern than Ton Lamyai, and no less lively.

Angels at the base of Wat Phra Singh library

2. Temples of the Old City

A samlor or tuk-tuk tour of Wat Phra Singh, Wat Chedi Luang, Wat Pan Tao, Wat Duang Di, Wat Chiang Man.

Flag down a *samlor* or, if you are impatient or pity the straining driver, a motorised *tuk-tuk*. As with all forms of local transport, do not pay the first price asked. Bargain. If you feel really energetic, take a *tuk-tuk* to Wat Phra Singh and walk to the others, a total distance of about 2km (1½ miles).

Even from a distance, **Wat Phra Singh**, Chiang Mai's most famous temple after Wat Phra That Doi Suthep, is impressive. Sited at the T-intersection of Ratchdamneon and Singharat roads, its *viharn*, just beyond the entrance gate, is stately.

Like many Lanna temples of northern Thailand, Wat Phra Singh has a balustrade that depicts a *naga* (serpent) with a *makara* emerging from its mouth. This is a motif commonly favoured by Khmer artists in the

Samlor driver taking a break

The sacred gum tree of Wat Chedi Luang

temples of Thailand's northeast. The Buddha inside is rather ordinary but the ornate wood and mosaic pulpit on the left is worth a closer examination.

Exit the *viharn,* turn left to the beautiful library, a wooden Lanna-style building erected on an older base. Its stucco angels convey a tranquillity and delicacy matched only by those at Wat Jet Yot.

Directly behind the *viharn* is a beautiful wooden *bot* with a stunning stucco and gold entrance. Behind it is a *chedi* built by King Pha Yu in 1345 to hold the ashes of his father, King Kam Fu. In Sukhothai (and Sri Lankan) tradition, the structure rests on the backs of four brick and stucco elephants, one on each side.

The most beautiful building in the temple compound is the famous **Phra Viharn Laikam** to the left of the *chedi.* As typical of a *bot,* its area of sanctuary is defined by six *bai sema,* or boundary stones, except that these are phallic-shaped. Of all of Chiang Mai's temple buildings, this is perhaps the most representative of Lanna-style architecture although it was built in 1811, rather late in the Lanna period. Intricately carved stucco door frames compete for attention with the doors, which are dominated by lacquer guardians.

Inside the Phra Viharn Laikam are murals painted in the 19th century. The one on the right wall tells the story of *Saengthong,* an ancient Thai tale with little boys, buffaloes, and other delightful characters from 200 years ago. On the left wall is the story of the *Suphannahong,* a mythical swan which is an important figure in northern art and architecture. Unfortunately, the mural is so badly damaged by water that the images are almost indistinct. If you peer closely enough, you can make out enough of the mural to have some idea of the grandeur of the original.

Exit Wat Phra Singh and head for **Wat Chedi Luang**, one of Chiang Mai's most impressive temples. Located on Phra Pokklao

The viharn gables of Wat Chedi Luang

Road, the fate of the tall gum tree just inside the entrance is linked to that of the city: according to legend, when the gum tree falls, so will Chiang Mai. The tree shades the city pillar which traditionally marks the geographic centre of a Thai town and from which the power that guards its inhabitants emanates.

The temple's *viharn* is rather plain, holding a tall Standing Buddha flanked by two disciples. Of more interest are the framed pictures along the walls with English-language captions explaining the story of the Buddha's life. These are worth reviewing in order to understand similar paintings found in other Chiang Mai temples.

The temple's most impressive structure is the huge *chedi* at the rear. Built in 1401 by King Saeng Muang Ma and raised to a height of 86m (282ft) by King Tilokaraja (the builder of Wat Jet Yot) in 1454, the *chedi* was reduced to its present height of 42m (138ft) by a massive earthquake in 1545. Unfortunately, the Fine Arts Department, which handled the restoration of the ruined *chedi* – an object of great beauty and which the people of Chiang Mai loved and revered – did a poor job, managing to create one of the ugliest edifices for miles around.

The restored Wat Chedi Luang

In contrast, the *viharn* of **Wat Pan Tao**, next door to Wat Chedi Luang, is a masterpiece of wood construction. Visible from the street, its fire-engine red doorway is crowned by a lovely Lanna peacock framed by golden serpents.

Continue down Phra Pokklao Road to a small *soi* (lane) on the right just before the corner of Ratchawithi Road and the Provincial Law Court. Here, **Wat Duang Di**, made up of three Northern Thai wooden temples, offers little but is a pleasant stop along this tour.

Wat Chiang Man on Rajapakinai Road is the oldest of the four principal temples within the city walls. Built in 1296, the year Chiang Mai was founded, its name translates as 'power of the city' suggesting its importance to Chiang Mai's early inhabitants. The courtyard is thought to have served as the home of King Mengrai while he was building his new capital. Its Lanna-style *viharn*, dating from the 19th century, is decorated with an intricately-carved, three-headed elephant god, Erawan, as well as some superbly carved teak panels on the gable. Inside the *viharn* are several handsome

bronze Buddha images from the Lanna and U-thong periods. If the temple is not open, ask one of the monks for the key.

The *viharn* on the right contains Chiang Mai's two most sacred Buddha images. The most important is the 10-cm (4-inch) high **Phra Setang Khamani** on the left, a small crystal Buddha image brought from Lamphun – where it had been for over 600 years – to Chiang Mai by King Mengrai in 1281. The image is said to command the clouds, and during a drought, Chiang Mai residents propitiate it to bring rain. On the festive day of Songkran, the image is carried around the city in a grand procession and water is poured over it to invite the rains in the coming rice-planting season. The image is also thought to protect the city from fire.

A second image, the finely-carved **Phra Sila**, on the right side of the altar, is thought to have been brought from India, or Sri Lanka around the end of the first millenium. On the *viharn* walls are murals depicting the Life of Buddha on the upper panels and the *chadoks* (previous incarnations of Buddha) on the lower panels.

Of particular interest is the 15th-century square *chedi* at the rear of the temple compound. Reflecting Sri Lankan and Sukhothai tradition, the *chedi* appears to be supported on the backs of 15 stone elephants built into the base of the structure, as is found in several Sukhothai and Kampaengphet *chedi*.

Look also at the *ho trai*, or library, containing Buddhist scriptures. It sits to the left of the *chedi* and is a masterpiece of wood carving and lacquer decoration. In the Central Plains of Thailand, a structure

The chedi sitting atop 15 stone elephants at Wat Chiang Man

like this would sit atop columns in a pond so that the sacred manuscripts would not be eaten by termites. The library holds a small museum with lacquer manuscript cabinets, Buddha images, pipes and old Thai money. In the far left-hand corner of the compound, the plain, wide wooden doors of the *bot* conceal some superb Lanna and U-thong period bronze Buddha images.

3. Temples Beyond Chiang Mai

Visit some of the more stately temples on the outskirts of Chiang Mai: Wat Suan Dok, Wat U-Mong, Wat Jet Yot, Wat Ku Tao, plus a stop at the Chiang Mai Museum.

Part of the appeal of the temples outside the city is their air of tranquillity which hearkens to an earlier, quieter age. Within their walls, you can experience the Buddhist calm the temples were originally invested with. The first of these lies on the left along Suthep Road (*songthaews* heading west out of Suan Dok Gate will take you there). Get off at the temple gate 300m (330yds) beyond the traffic lights.

Founded in 1383, **Wat Suan Dok** (the Flower Garden Temple) is originally thought to have been a royal pleasure garden. Legend says that the Sri Lankan monk Sumana was directed in a dream

Wat Ku Tao

Chattering Monks

While wandering around temples, you may be approached by young monks asking innumerable questions. Their interest is in practising English but they are often also a fount of information about village life (many are country boys) and daily temple routines. Unless they are clutching books soliciting donations, take a few moments to talk to them. Such encounters can often lead to insights about life in Thailand.

to dig beneath an old *chedi* in Sukhothai. His shovel unearthed a series of boxes within boxes, the innermost containing a glowing gem. When the Sukhothai king attempted to use the gem's miraculous powers for his own gain, it stopped glowing. Sumana then took it to Chiang Mai where King Ku Na erected a *chedi* in his flower garden to hold it. As it was being buried, the gem split in two, much to everyone's consternation. One half was then buried in the *chedi* and the other half transported on elephant back to Doi Suthep, where a second *chedi* was built.

Recent restoration of the *viharn* has resulted in a cold shell of concrete and iron grills. Even this, however, fails to detract from the beauty of its 500-year-old Buddha image. It is in the courtyard to the west, however, that its true appeal lies. Here, next to an elegant *chedi* built in 1372 and restored in 1931, is a garden of several brilliant white *chedi* containing the ashes of Chiang Mai nobles, an impressive sight at any hour of the day.

Continue along Suthep Road through the Ton Payom market area, cross the canal and after 500m (550yds) turn left for Wat U-

Mong, 1km (½ mile) away. In the days when the valley floor was covered in forests and travel was difficult, **Wat U-Mong** was a quiet meditation retreat, a quality it has maintained to this day. Recently restored, it sits among stately teak trees that evoke a sense of peace. Sit for a while and listen to the leaves rustling and the cicadas singing. Next door is an open zoo.

Return to Suthep Road, turn right and at the second lot of traffic lights, turn left into Nimmanhamin Road. Cross over the intersection at the Amari Rincome Hotel corner on to the Superhighway, and after 1km (½ mile), turn left again to enter **Wat Jet Yot**.

Founded by King Tilokaraja in 1455, this unusual structure is a replica of the Mahabodi Temple in Bodhgaya, India, where Buddha gained enlightenment. Soon after the completion of the temple, Tilokaraja arranged for the 8th World Buddhist Council to meet in

Wat U-Mong sits amidst solitude

Chiang Mai in 1477. The meeting was attended by more than one hundred monks from various countries. In 1566, however, Wat Jet Yot was badly damaged when the Burmese conquered Chiang Mai and pillaged it.

The **Chiang Mai Museum** (Wednesday to Sunday 9am–4pm) on the Superhighway near Wat Jet Yot provides a superb overview of Lanna art. Among its prize exhibits is a huge Chiang Saen-style bronze Buddha head 3m (10ft) tall and a beautiful footprint inlaid with intricate mother-of-pearl. The museum also offers a catholic representation of Northern artefacts ranging from hilltribe costumes to items used in the everyday life of the hilltribes.

Continue along the Superhighway to Chang Pheuak Road, turn right and then left on Soi 6, opposite Thai Thanu Bank. **Wat Ku Tao** is at the end of the lane behind a wall guarded by celestial lions. The temple's *viharn* is plain but the unusual *chedi* commands attention. People disagree on whether it resembles five pumpkins or five alms bowls in descending size, stacked atop each other. Look closely at the flowers and foliage fashioned from ceramic shards. Although this is a functioning temple, with monks and lay worshippers much in evidence, one of Wat Ku Tao's main attractions is its tranquility. Sit under the banyan tree and contemplate its peace.

Wat Suan Dok

Excursions

4. Chiang Dao and the Ping River

Watch pachyderms at work at Chiang Dao Elephant Camp then raft down the Ping River. If you have your own car, continue to Chiang Dao caves.

A bus leaves the Chang Pheuak Gate Bus Station at 7am, crossing a flat valley and climbing the northern valley wall. Farm houses and neat squares of rice or vegetable fields line either side of the road. Soon, the bus is twisting and turning along the bends high above the beautiful Ping River (see map on page 52/53).

Tell the driver you want to get off at KM56 (watch the kilometre posts along the road). You will arrive at the **Chiang Dao Elephant Camp** in time for the 9am show; if you take the 7.30am bus, watch the 10am show instead. The show begins with a majestic procession of elephants up the Ping River. Then it is bath time with much splashing and trumpeting. Later, the elephants demonstrate how they move large teak logs as if they were matchsticks, a skill they have employed for more than a century in the teak forests of the North. After the 40-minute show, guests are invited to take a short elephant-back amble around the grounds. Perched high in a wooden howdah you gain a unique view of the scenery and an impressive close-up view of the huge beast's musculature and thick hide.

After the show, have a snack at the open air restaurant overlooking the Ping River and then negotiate with boatmen for the 4-km (2½-mile) ride on a bamboo raft down the **Ping River** to **Tha Rua**. The narrow raft can hold four persons with a boatman paddling the craft on a leisurely 45-minute journey through tropical vegetation and, quite appropriately, elephant grass.

At the journey's end, walk the short distance to the Chiang Mai-Fang Highway

Chiang Dao Elephant Camp

Entrance to the Chiang Dao Caves

and hail a bus for the ride to Chiang Mai. If you had driven and parked at the Elephant Camp, catch a bus to retrieve your vehicle and then head up the highway to Chiang Dao. About 500m (550yds) beyond the town, turn left 5km (3 miles) through villages and tobacco fields to the **Chiang Dao caves**.

The caves are a series of rooms reached by climbing stairs and, in one instance, a ladder through a narrow passage. Pay the entrance fee and get a guide to accompany you. The caves extend for more than 10km (6 miles), but do not attempt to explore beyond the Reclining Buddha, a good 10-minute walk away. Return to your vehicle, stop for a drink under the tamarind trees and then return to Chiang Mai. Several shops along the way sell farm implements, fishing baskets, and other village utensils. These make unusual gifts.

5. Mae Sa Valley

This varied day takes you through a beautiful valley to visit its attractions: an elephant camp, an orchid nursery and butterfly farm, and an old museum.

Hire a car or a motorcycle for the day. Travel south on H108 for 16km (10 miles) towards Hang Dong, then turn right onto H1269, travelling for 2km (1¼ miles) to **Wat Ton Kwen** on the left (a roadside sign indicates the turning). This peaceful little temple amid palm trees is a lovely example of Lanna architecture. The wooden *bot*, guarded by a pair of handsome stucco *naga*, is surrounded on three sides by an open cloister, an unusual architectural treatment. Take a close look at the especially fine decoration on the *bot* and the *viharn* in front of it.

H1269 loops around behind Doi Suthep. At KM38, where there is a police booth on the left, continue straight down the hill into **Samoeng**, a pretty valley town with some lovely, tree-shaded back streets. Have an iced coffee in a roadside restaurant and return to KM38, turning left onto H1096 at the police booth.

After 14km (8¼ miles), pass through Pong Yang Village and at KM13 enter the top of the Mae Sa Valley Resort. Take a break to stretch your legs, admire the flowers and have some refreshments. At KM10 you will reach the site of the **Mae Sa Elephant Camp**, with daily shows at 8am and 9.40am. Visitors can watch elephants bathing, dragging logs and performing other feats. With an early start you might catch the 9.40am show. If you are a late starter, do this itinerary anticlockwise and visit Mae Sa Valley first, taking in the 8am elephant show before continuing to complete the Samoeng loop in a more leisurely manner. At KM7 look out for **Mae Rim Orchid Nursery**. Dozens of varieties of orchids are nurtured under netting. One can buy seedlings with full instructions for their care — but check plant quarantine regulations if you plan on taking the seedlings out to another country.

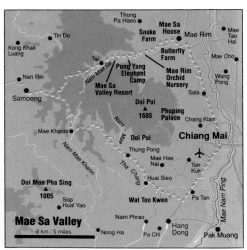

The **Mae Sa Snake Farm** is at KM3, and a bit further on you will see a board pointing to the Mae Sa Bronze Foundry, just before Lanna House Antiques and Handicrafts. Opposite the Shell petrol station is a large parking lot in front of the **Mae Sa Butterfly Farm**. The butterfly farm raises a large variety of beautiful butterflies in a spacious garden setting. The farm has a shop which sells framed specimens, although after seeing them flying so freely you may not have the heart to buy them stretched out for display on cotton. Also for sale are a wide variety of exquisite orchids grown on the farm as well as jewellery made from live orchids and other flowers which have been electroplated in gold.

Further down the road is the **Mae Sa House** (open daily 8am–5pm). Were it not for the Thai setting, you would have thought that the museum was somewhere in Europe, since a number of the exhibits are family heirlooms collected on trips abroad.

Apart from European artefacts, the Thai-style house contains a collection of Sukothai ceramics and amusing items like a clock that runs backwards and there is also an early model of a motorcycle.

Wat Ton Kwen

To return to Chiang Mai, you drive along H 1096 for another 3km (1¾ miles) to H 108. You then turn right and within 16km (5 miles) you will enter Chiang Mai through Chang Pheuak Gate.

ฟาร์มผีเสื้อ แม่สา

MAESA BUTTERFLY FARM

Lamphun

to Chiang Mai

Moat

Kwang River

to Wat Chamathewi

Museum

Wat Phra That
Haripunchai

Footbridge

Wat Prayoon

to Lampang

Kwang River

Moat

A ride through a corridor of beautiful gum trees to the quiet old capital of the 7th-century Haripunchai Empire.

Lamphun, the old capital of the Haripunchai Empire, lies 26km (16 miles) south of Chiang Mai. To get there, hire a motorbike or take a bus from the stop on the Chiang Mai-Lamphun Road, about 200m (220yds) south of the Nawarat Bridge. This is one of the prettiest drives in the kingdom: just south of Chiang Mai, the Chiang Mai-Lamphun Road runs between twin rows of magnificent tall gum trees – planted 130 years ago by the Prince of Chiang Mai – all the way to the border with the Lamphun Province.

Lamphun is a small town of spacious lawns. Its principal temple, **Wat Phra That Haripunchai**, founded in 1044 atop the site of a ruined royal palace, lies between the main street and the river. Al-though its entrance, guarded by two lions, faces the river on the eastern side, most visitors enter the temple through the western gate from the main street.

The first major structure you encounter is a stepped pyramidal *chedi* with niches containing images of the Standing Buddha. You will note a resemblance to Wat Chedi Liem (see *Itinerary 7*) and the *chedi* of nearby Wat Chamathewi of which this is a replica. There are several other *chedi* of similar design found throughout northern parts of Thailand.

The dominant structure in the wide temple courtyard is a 50-m (164-ft) tall Lanna *chedi* covered in gold leaf. The original *chedi* was built in 1467; subsequent reno-vations raised it to its pre-

Wat Phra That Haripunchai

sent height. Next to it is a *viharn* whose principal appeal is its lovely doors. Restored in 1925 after a fire, the *viharn* contains a fine bronze Chiang Saen Buddha image.

Wandering around the temple grounds you will see an impressive bronze gong hanging under a large bell. The gong, northern Thailand's largest, was cast in 1860, and the bell, four years later.

Exit from the eastern gate and cross the road and the foot-bridge over the Kwang River, a branch of the Ping River (in fact, the original channel before it shifted). This farming area holds **Wat Prayoon** with its Burmese-style *chedi* atop a former *mondop*, or square reliquary, built in 1369.

When sated, return to the main street, turn left and walk to the corner. Cross the street to reach the **Lamphun National Museum** (Wednesday to Sunday 9am–4pm), which contains a fine collection

Wat Haripunchai's bronze gong

of bronze images from Wat Phra That the and surrounding temples.

Walk or take a *samlor* to **Wat Chamathewi**, 1km (½ mile) to the west across the moat and past Wat Mahawan. The temple is unspectacular save for a pair of unusual brick and stucco *chedi* next to the *viharn* in the wide, tree-lined courtyard. Especially interesting is the larger square stepped-pyramid *chedi* built in 1218, on which the one in Wat Phra That Haripunchai is modelled. The *chedi* is made up of five tiers, each divided into three niches. Each niche holds a Standing Buddha statue in it, making an impressive display of 15 Buddha images on each of the four sides of the pyramid. The stucco Buddha images are crafted in the Dvaravati style, characterised by their diaphanous robes, and elongated ears and tranquil expressions etched on wide faces.

Wat Chamathewi, also referred to as Wat Kukut, is named after its legendary 7th-century Mon queen founder, Chamathewi, whose ashes, it is said, are contained in the square stepped-pyramid *chedi*. According to popular myth, Queen Chamathewi, while pregnant, left her husband for reasons unknown and headed north from Lavo (Lopburi) to build a new city. On the banks of the Kwang River, however, she had to stop to give birth to twin sons. Here, she gave instructions for a city protected by a rectangular moat to be built. Called Haripunchai, the name of the city was later changed to Lamphun. The remains of that early period are found at Wat Chamathewi, which, oddly enough, was built outside the protective confines of the city wall.

Return to Chiang Mai by bus. They run every five minutes, with the last bus leaving at 7pm.

Motorcycle Jaunts

The beauty of a motorcycle is that it can take you to places where cars cannot go. Despite the wealth of roads that have been constructed in the North, there are still lots of dirt tracks requiring a 125 c.c. trailbike and sufficient riding skills. If you do not know how to ride a motorcycle, do not attempt to learn in Thailand. Slippery roads, crazy dogs that dart across the highway, buffaloes and people that meander along it, and deep potholes all conspire to befuddle the unwary rider. If you are not confident of your riding ability, take the motorcycle on one of the easier trips outlined in this book. There will still be plenty of challenges and you will be able to concentrate on the scenery instead of fighting the bike.

7. Wat Chedi Liem and Baan Tawai

A motorbike tour to Wat Chedi Liem and along the Ping River through countryside to Baan Tawai, the village of instant antiques.

Head south along the Chiang Mai-Lamphun Road. As you enter the corridor of tall trees that line the sides of the road there is a junction with traffic lights. About 2km (1¼ mile) past it is a 'Y' intersection: take the right fork, marked by the sign: Ban Nong Hoi. About 1 km (½ mile) farther on is **Wat Chedi Liem**. Similar to that in Lamphun's Wat Chamathewi, this *chedi* was built by Chiang Mai's founder, King Mengrai, who must have seen the original when he conquered Lamphun in 1281. Mengrai, who built it in honour of his queen who died in 1283, donated the *chedi* to the temple on its completion in 1288.

About 1km (½ mile) farther on, when the road forks again at a big banyan tree that stands before a temple, take the right fork to **Saraphi Dam**. Cross the narrow iron bridge and turn left on the other side. Continue 2km (1¼ miles) to a four-way intersection. Turn right here and and ride through fields for another 2km (1¼ miles) or so to get to Baan Tawai.

Baan Tawai village is little more than a corridor of woodcarving workshops, with artisans producing the 'new' antiques found in the handicraft shops of Chiang Mai. The yards of these workhops are piled high with wooden handicrafts. You can pick up some good bargains but getting a metre-tall wooden elephant home on your motorcycle is going to require a bit of ingenuity. Approach one of several shippers who have set up shop in the village instead.

To return, continue through Baan Tawai to **Hang Dong**. Turn right onto the Chiang Mai-Hot highway (H 108) and, a few kilometres later, arrive back in Chiang Mai.

Map:
Baan Tawai
10 km / 6 miles
Chiang Mai
Ton Kuk
Ton
Mae Hae Nai
Tamna
Huai Sieo
Tom
Khun Se
Pa Tan
Wat Chedi Liem
Saraphi
Nam Phrao
Hang Dong
Chang Kham
Pak Muang
Saraphi Dam
Pa Chi
Baan Tawai
Han Kaeo
Rong Dua
San Pa Tong
Kuan
Ping River
Pratu Pa Luang
San Khayom
Pa Yang
Nong Pla Siu
Lamphun
Sop Pa

Baan Tawai, wooden carvings

8. Back Country Biking

By motorbike to Chom Thong, Mae Klang Waterfalls, Doi Inthanon and back via Mae Chaem, Ob Luang Gorge and Hot.

Leave Chiang Mai on H108, and head for Chom Thong 58km (36 miles) south. **Chom Thong** holds the handsome **Wat Phra That Si Chom Thong** with its beautiful gilded *chedi* that dates from 1451. The large cruciform *viharn*, built in 1516, contains a collection of fine bronze images and Buddha images carved on elephant tusks. Behind the principal Buddha is a small museum.

Have a drink at the restaurant next to the temple, then return to the head of the town and turn left for the road to **Doi Inthanon**. Some 7km (4¼ miles) down on the left is the lovely **Mae Klang Waterfall**. At KM8 is the entrance to the park, and just past it the Visitor's Centre where you can buy a detailed map of the park and a bird-watching book that lists the over 360 species of birds that are frequently seen here.

The road then climbs through pine forests to the checkpost at KM38 and then up a steep slope that is mostly shrouded by rain and mists during the monsoon season. At KM49, the 2,565m (8,400ft) summit, is a shrine to Chao Inthanon, a former prince of Chiang Mai, after which the mountain is named. The views from the summit

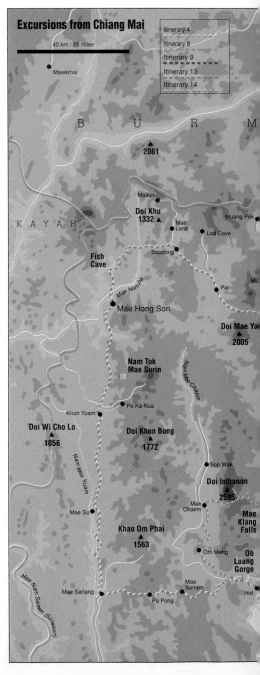

Excursions from Chiang Mai

40 km / 25 miles

Itinerary 4
Itinerary 8
Itinerary 9
Itinerary 13
Itinerary 14

Mawkmai

B   U   R   M

2061

Mailun

Doi Khu
1332

Mae Lana

Muang Pok

Lod Cave

K A Y A H

Fish Cave

Soppong

Mae Nam Pai

Pai

Mae Hong Son

Doi Mae Ya
2005

Nam Tok Mae Surin

Nam Mae Chaem

Po Ka Nua

Khun Yuam

Doi Wi Cho Lo
1056

Doi Khun Bong
1772

Nam Mae Yuam

Sop Wak

Doi Inthanon
2595

Mae Su

Mae Chaem

Khao Om Phai
1563

Mae Klang Falls

Om Meng

Ob Luang Gorge

Mae Nam Salawin (Salween)

Mae Sariang

Pa Pong

Mae Sanam

Hot

are somewhat disappointing, even in good weather. Go down the mountain for the best viewpoint at KM41, marked by two remarkable *chedi* built by the Royal Thai Air Force to honour King Bhumibol and Queen Sirikit. These remarkable structures, which stand amidst carefully tended gardens of temperate flowers and vegetables, must rank amongst the most architecturally innovative buildings of their kind anywhere in Thailand. Particularly noteworthy are the mod-

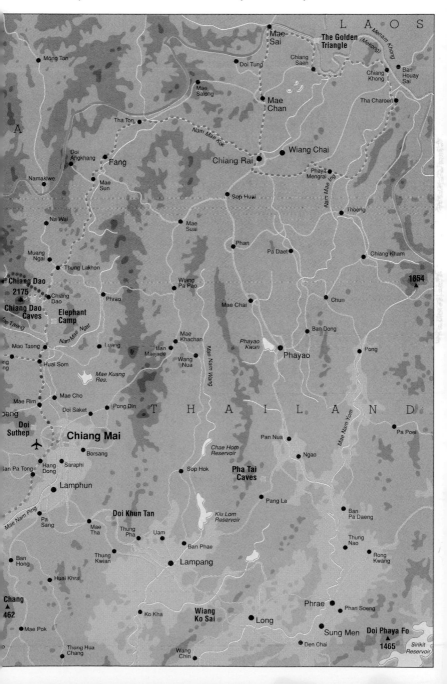

Mae Klang waterfalls

ernistic interpretations of traditional Buddhist themes portrayed in copper-coloured tiles on the face of the King's *chedi*. The same is true of the elaborate interior murals of the Queen's *chedi*, which are reminiscent − in a Buddhist sense − of the controversial style first unveiled at Coventry Cathedral in England. In borders nearby fuchsias, salvias, petunias, hydrangeas and helicrishams blend unexpectedly with decorative cabbages, adding to the unique charm of the location.

At KM38, just before the checkpoint, turn right into H1192. The one-lane road winds through some of the greenest and most beautiful forests in Thailand. Take your time both to enjoy the scenery and take photographs, and to negotiate the tight bends and steep descents. The road eventually opens into the Mae Chaem Valley and 22km (13¾ miles) later arrives at a 'Y' intersection. Take the right-hand fork into the town of **Mae Chaem** where you can stop to have lunch.

To return to Chiang Mai, backtrack to the Y intersection 1km (½ mile) before entering the town and take the right fork to H1088. After 45km (28 miles) you reach the main road (H108) between Mae Sariang and Hot. Turn left towards Hot, about 22km (13¾ miles) away. A few kilometres further, you reach **Ob Luang Gorge**, billed as 'Thailand's Grand Canyon', a grand overstatement but worth a stop for a quick look and a drink. There is little to see in **Hot** but it does have a motorcycle repair shop, if you need one, and gas station on the north end of town. After filling up, head north up H108 and into Chiang Mai.

Tips For Motorcyclists

Protect yourself by renting a helmet, wearing solid shoes, not sandals, and checking before you rent a bike that the brakes, horn, lights and signals are in proper working order. Drive defensively by flashing your lights when you see a car trying to overtake another in an on-coming lane.

Rental bikes are often not well-maintained but you should not compound the problem by using dirty or improper fuel. While the small petrol pumps along the road are picturesque, use them only in emergencies as the petrol they sell is often adulturated. It is better to fill up at an established petrol station. Make sure you carry extra clothes since they will quickly soak up all the dirt and dust your wheels will kick up.

If you plan to do a lot of motorbiking, contact David Unkovich (the Golden Triangle Rider) by fax at 219 211 or email: davidfl@cm.ksc.co.th You can rent well-maintained motorcycles, plus accessories like a helmet, gloves and jacket here, besides collecting maps and obtaining useful information and many hints that will help you plan your trip.

9. Chiang Dao Mountain

A trailbike ride behind Thailand's third highest mountain (2,175m/7,136ft) on dirt roads. This trail is for experienced bikers only.

Just beyond the market in Chiang Dao is a Shell station; fill up as you will need a full tank for this route. Take the road to the left, which leads 5km (3 miles) past tobacco fields to the base of **Doi Chiang Dao** (see map on page 52/53). Here, the road forks but you should continue straight ahead to visit the interesting **Chi-**

A hilltribe village near Chiang Dao

ang Dao caves (see *Pick & Mix 4*) if you haven't seen them already. Once you've explored enough of the caves, which contain unusual rock formations and assorted Buddha images – the caves are a popular pilgrimage area for monks – backtrack about 100m (110yds) or so and take the right-hand fork that you by-passed earlier.

The dirt road crosses cotton fields shaded by tall gum trees and after a checkpost begins to climb. About 12km (7½ miles) up the road, a fork to the left will take you to **Baan Na Lao Mai**, a Lisu village behind Doi Chiang Dao. Continue another 35km (21¾ miles) to the Karen village of **Muang Khong** on the banks of the Mae Taeng River. The route is steep and may be impassable after rainfall. The rewards, though, for persevering are beautiful forests and spectacular mountain scenery.

Chiang Dao in the early morning light

A bicycle tour of this northerly city's two main temples: Wat Phra Singh and Wat Phra Kaeo.

Chiang Rai, the capital of Thailand's most northerly province, is 180km (112 miles) from Chiang Mai by Route 118. In addition to two daily Thai Airways flights from Chiang Mai to Chiang Rai, it is also possible to fly directly from Bangkok. Apart from being a good base for trekking and hilltribe visits, there is not much of interest in Chiang Rai. Rent a bicycle for this tour.

There are numerous temples in Chiang Rai but only two rate close examination. The first is **Wat Phra Singh** on a short road that passes the central post office and links Singhalai and Uttarakit roads. This modern temple is distinguished by a pair of doors designed and carved by Thawan Duchanee, a local artist who became renowned in Bangkok and later in Germany. The doors are typical of his visceral style and the guardians are fierce enough to frighten away any demon. It says something about the liberality of the abbot that the guardians both don penises, one in the shape of a serpent and the other, an elephant's head.

The second temple is **Wat Phra Kaeo** on Trairat Road between Ruang Nakorn and Singhalai roads. The temple is believed to have been the original residence of the Emerald Buddha, which is kept in the royal temple of the same name in Bangkok. A fine example of Lanna-style architecture, the *viharn* has lacquered doors and a carved wooden gable. The image inside is from the Chiang Saen period and probably dates from the 15th century.

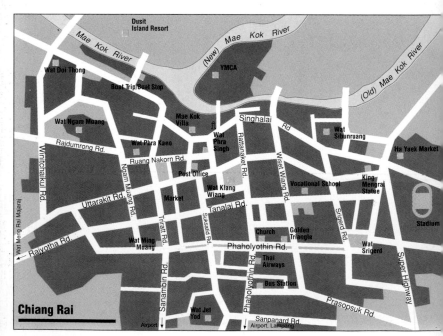

56

Wat Phra Singh, Chiang Rai

Call in at the nearby **Tourist Authority of Thailand** (TAT) office at 448/16 Singhalai (tel: 717433), near the YMCA for information to help you plan the rest of your visit.

For a longer bike ride, travel upstream along the bank of the **Mae Kok River** beyond the Dusit Island Resort. At the base of Doi Tong cross the Mae Kah Luang Bridge and explore the countryside and a village close to a limestone peak. On the way back take a dip in the Dusit Thani hotel pool for a small fee or a snack in the coffee shop.

Spend the afternoon and evening contacting a trekking agency – and perhaps other travellers – to arrange a one-day tour to hilltribe villages for the following day (see *Excusrion 12*).

Chiang Rai city pillars

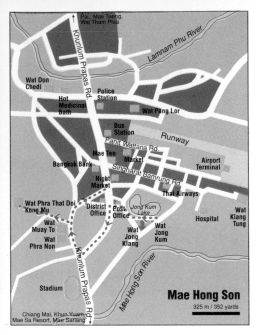

Pai, Mae Taeng,
Wat Tham Plaa

Lamnam Phu River

Khunlum Prapas Rd.

Wat Don
Chedi

Hot
Medicinal
Bath

Police
Station

Wat Pang Lor

Bus
Station

Panit Wattana Rd.

Runway

Mae Tee

Market

Bangkok Bank

Singharat Bamrung Rd.

Airport
Terminal

Night
Market

Thai Airways

Wat Phra That Doi
Kong Mu

District
Office

Post
Office

Jong Kum
Lake

Wat
Kiang
Tung

Wat
Muay To

Wat
Jong
Klang

Wat
Jong
Kum

Hospital

Wat
Phra Non

Khunlum Prapas Rd.

Mae Hong Son River

Stadium

Mae Hong Son

325 m / 352 yards

Chiang Mai, Khun Yuam,
Mae Sa Resort, Mae Sariang

11. Mae Hong Son

Soak in the atmosphere of this town on the Burmese border. Besides being an excellent base for trekking, Mae Hong Son's highlights include Wat Jong Klang, Wat Jong Kum, Wat Phra Non, and the village of Huay Poo Gaeng, where the famous 'long-necked' Padaung women live.

Don't bother with the 11-hour, 368-km (230-mile) bus journey from Chiang Mai to Mae Hong Son since it costs so little to fly. Thai Airways offers four daily 40-minute flights from Chiang Mai to Mae Hong Son, but note that flights are sometimes disrupted by rain and heavy mists. If you travel during the winter season, pack warm clothing as the nights can get very cold. There is a noticeable absence of public transportation in Mae Hong Son. When I asked a man how people got around town, he looked at me puzzled and said 'We walk' as if nothing could be more obvious. So start walking.

Lying in a forested valley, Mae Hong Son rightly deserves its sobriquet 'Valley of Mists' because of its early morning fog and cloud-covered hills. On particularly bad days, the peaks are covered by grey clouds and blanketed by curtains of falling rain. The only time the mists let up is between November and March, the best time to visit. Mae Hong Son is also known for the fact that it lies on the Burmese-Thai border smuggling routes. Once a quiet, peaceful province housing various ethnic groups including the Karen, Meo, Lawa, Shan, Lisu and Burmese, Mae Hong Son now brims with activity: new hotels and guesthouses, and numerous trekking agencies catering to the tourist trade.

Get a room in a hotel in the vicinity of Jong Kum Lake, like the Piya Guest House, the up-market Baiyoke Chalet, or a budget guesthouse like Rose Garden.

Jong Kum Lake mirroring Wat Jong Klang

58

As it will probably be early afternoon when you arrive, spend some time just soaking up the atmosphere at **Jong Kum Lake**. There is a fitness park around the lake if you feel like working out. Visit the two temples that fringe the lake: **Wat Jong Klang** and **Wat Jong Kum**. Both are fine examples of Burmese architecture with their tiny roofs stacked one atop the other and filigree woodwork along the eaves. The *chedi*, too, is a prime example of Burmese design with its terraced base, squat body, and spire of discs rising to a delicate crown representing a sacred umbrella shading a holy relic.

A shrine at Wat Jong Klang

Wat Jong Klang has a fine collection of statues and glass paintings depicting scenes from the *Vessantara Chadok*, which tells the story of the last incarnation of the man who, in his next life, would become the Buddha.

In the afternoon, walk to **Wat Phra Non** and its 12-m (31-ft) long Reclining Buddha image, the position the Buddha assumed when he died. Cross the street and brace yourself; you are about

Padaung woman weaving cloth

to climb a stairway as difficult as that which ascends Chiang Mai's Doi Suthep. It leads to **Wat Phra That Doi Kong Mu**, but the unfit may prefer to take a *tuk tuk* up the road. The *wat* comprises two beautiful *chedi* and a commanding view of the surrounding countryside. Walk to the parapet on the eastern rim to watch the sun set over the town and the mountains. Few views are as impressive as this. Descend the stairs. For dinner, walk to the **night market** on Kunlumprapas Road and order Thai food from the stalls. Before returning to your hotel, stroll down to the lake to enjoy the tiny lights on the *chedi* of Wat Jong Klang as they reflect off the water's surface.

The next morning, rise early to watch the sunrise and to see why Mae Hong Son is called the 'Valley of Mists'. Rise before dawn and walk to the lake's edge to watch the reflection of Wat Jong Klang on the shimmering water and the barefoot monks in their saffron robes padding along on their morning alms walk. Then, watch the sun melt away the fog and reveal the *wat* in its full splendour. Take a short walk to the nearby market for breakfast before continuing with the rest of the tour.

Hire a *tuk tuk* to the boat landing about 6km (3¾ miles) south of town past the Mae Hong Son Resort. There, bargain with a boatman to take you to the village of **Huay Poo Gaeng** near the Burmese border to visit the Burmese Padaung tribe – also referred to as the Long-Necked Karen – refugees from their native Burma because of the civil war. Now the subject of gawking tourists, the Padaung women are well known for wearing heavy brass rings around their necks, a practice that starts from 5 or 6 years old and is considered attractive by Padaung men. The concentric brass rings, which can weigh as much as 5kg (11lbs), give the women the appearance of having long necks, but in reality, the rings do not so much stretch the necks as depress the collarbones.

In the afternoon, hire a *tuk tuk* (or catch the bus to Pai) to go to **Wat Tham Plaa**, 17km (10½ miles) up H1095 towards Pai. Get off and turn left at a sign that says 'Fish Cave' and walk 200m (218yds) to a narrow suspension bridge. Cross it and five minutes later arrive at the cave. Next to it is a pool bubbling from a subterranean stream. The pool holds a variety of fish that grows up to 1m (3½ft) in length. Feed them with bread bought at the park official's hut.

Return to Mae Hong Son and spend the evening shopping for Burmese *kalaga* tapestries and lacquerware at **Singharat Bamrung Road**; the La-or Shop in particular has a wide selection.

Dine at the **Fern Restaurant**, just downhill from the Post Office. The restaurant is run by former graduates of Chulalongkorn University and serves excellent Thai food.

Yao women in their tribal finery

12. Hilltribe Treks

Hilltribe treks are the reason why many people visit the north of Thailand. Treks range from half a day to a week or more.

When hilltribe treks were introduced two decades ago, few tourists went on them, so their impact on minority villages and their cultures was minimal. Today, with dozens of companies operating hilltribe treks, the way of life of the hilltribes is changing irrevocably. Many agencies exploit the villages for commercial gain and the hilltribes in turn become dependant on a false economy.

You can help minimise the adverse effects of trekking by signing up with a reputable agency. There are dozens of companies in the main trekking centres of Chiang Mai, Chiang Rai and Mae Hong Son. Trying to recommend one over another is difficult as the quality of the trek is dependent as much on the guide – who frequently changes companies – as on the logistics. Shop around and ask some pointed questions to determine if the proprietors are merely cashing in on a popular moneymaking activity or whether they are genuinely sensitive to tribal beliefs and customs.

An important question to ask is the size of your trekking group. A group of more than six people can literally take over a small village. Try to find a trek that visits one or two tribal groups only, not skipping through one village after another in rapid succession. Equally important is finding an agency that employs tribesmen as guides, and one who speaks adequate English. Ask other tourists who have come back from trekking for personal recommendations. There is some an-

61

tipathy between the hilltribes and Thai guides in recent years and there have been accusations of cultural insensitivity. If your guide seems to understand little of the culture, find another agency. Do some research by visiting the **Tribal Research Centre** at Chiang Mai University, (Monday to Friday 9am–4pm). The centre displays costumes, utensils and weapons of major hilltribe groups with maps showing the locale of each and a library of books.

The duration of the trek can be as short as an easy half a day to a fairly strenuous week or more, involving travel by bus, raft, on elephant back and on foot. Popular trekking areas are due north of Chiang Mai, between Chiang Dao and Mae Salong, and the hills around Chiang Rai. In Mae Hong Son, the treks go right up to the Burmese border and Mae Sot.

In Chiang Mai, there are scores of trekking agencies along Tha Phae Road and Chaiyaphum Road. One, on Charoen Prathet Road, makes the painful offer: 'Visit Elephant Riding on Foot'. In Chiang Rai, agencies are found along Phaholyothin and Prem Wipak roads, and in Mae Hong Son, a number are found along Khunlum Prapas Road. Guesthouses also frequently organise treks.

Trekking Tips

Dress casually but adequately to protect skin from the burning sun. I have seen Western women sitting topless on a raft on a sunny day. This is not only insensitive but it is also asking for trouble. Jogging or walking shoes are sufficient for hilltribe trekking. Some agencies provide sleeping bags and mosquito nets; others require you to take your own. Check with the agency before booking. Carry a daypack with a change of clothes (two, if during the rainy season) wrapped in plastic bags, a raincoat, first aid kit and toiletries. Carry a canteen rather than plastic water bottles which often get discarded, creating an environmental problem. Canteens, ponchos, sleeping bags and other equipment are sold in shops at Chiang Mai's Manee Nopparat Road near the northeast corner of the city wall. As it can get surprisingly dry during the winter months use chapstick and moisturiser.

Don't drink untreated water, or eat uncooked vegetables and peeled fruits. Use Puritabs, available in most pharmacies, to purify drinking water. Inoculation against Hepatitis A and B is highly recommended. Malaria is prevalent. Don't put your faith completely in anti-malarial pills. Your best advice is to avoid being bitten by using plenty of repellent and a mosquito net. See a doctor and do not accept flu as a diagnosis if you develop a fever. Insist on a blood test and mention the possiblity of malaria to your doctor. Note: See the *Practical Information* chapter for more tips on health matters and on tribal etiquette.

A 3½-day excursion down the Kok River to Chiang Rai, Mae Sai and the Golden Triangle (Sop Ruak), Chiang Saen, Chiang Khong and back to Chiang Rai. Travel by local bus and rented car.

Catch the 6am or 7.20am bus from Chiang Mai's Chang Pheuak Bus Station for the four-hour journey to **Tha Ton** (see map on page 52/53). The road climbs out of the valley and along the beautiful Ping River. Past Chiang Dao, it runs through tall teak forests before entering the plains around Fang and from there to Tha Ton. On reaching the large bridge over the Mae Kok River, the road turns right and you will see boats tied up to the bank.

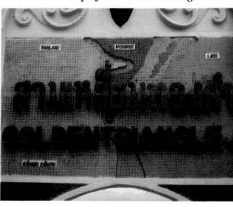

A mosaic map of the Golden Triangle

Boats leave for Chiang Rai for a set hire fee of 1,600 baht per boat, carrying up to eight passengers. Try to leave by 2pm. The four-hour journey down the **Kok River** to Chiang Rai takes you past hilltribe villages and grasslands. As it is a valley, there is little spectacular scenery or whitewater.

Spend the afternoon exploring **Chiang Rai** (see *Excursion 10*) by bicycle and then stay the night. The next morning, rent a car for two days and head for **Mae Sai**. Some 870km (540 miles) from Bangkok, Mae Sai is the northernmost point in Thailand. After passing rows of shophouses, the road ends at the **Sai River Bridge**. For some decades now the town has prospered, trading all kinds of goods from Burmese jade and antiques to coins and stamps.

The border with Burma, closed except to locals for almost 40 years, is now open to foreign visitors (Monday to Friday 8am–6pm), and day trips can be made to the Burmese border town of Tachilek. You need your passport, plus a photo-copy and US$10.

Stay in a hotel in Mae Sai or continue to the **Golden Triangle Hotel** (tel: 784001/5) in Sop Ruak, which lies at the apex of the **Golden Triangle** (Samliam Tong Kham), the point where Burma, Laos and Thailand meet. To get there, drive down H110 for about 300m (330yds) and turn left next to the Sin Wattana Hotel onto a paved road. It is another 34km (21 miles) to the Golden Triangle Hotel on the banks of the Mekong River and views of Burma and

Boat ride down Kok River

63

Boats for trips up the Mekong River

Laos. If this is too fancy for you, there are cheaper guesthouses farther along the road.

In the morning, have breakfast at the arch that demarcates the Golden Triangle and marvel at the fact that were there not a signpost, there would be nothing here to hold your interest, so ordinary is the landscape. The site marks the juncture of the borders of Thailand, Burma (Myanmar) and Laos and that is about it.

Rent a boat for a 25-minute cruise around the numerous small islands in the Mekong or pay slightly more to continue downriver to **Chiang Saen**. Catch a *tuk tuk* for the 9-km (5½-mile) journey back to the Golden Triangle arch to pick up your car, then drive back 11km (7 miles) to Chiang Saen.

Chiang Saen is one of the prettiest towns in the North principally because the city fathers have resisted the urge to modernise the town and cut down all its trees. Set on the banks of the Mekong, it is an important archaeological site, holding more than 130 ruins. The present city, thought to date from 1328, is built atop the ruins of an earlier settlement.

Drive down the road leading at right angles from the river towards Chiang Rai. Within a few hundred metres are the ruins of the city wall. Stop to examine it and the moat that was once filled by the waters of the Mekong. Just past the wall, turn right down a dirt road to **Wat Pasak**.

Pasak means 'teak forest' and while many of the trees are gone, those that remain give a particularly bucolic atmosphere to the site. The brick *chedi*, built in 1295 during the reign of Ramkhamhaeng of Sukhothai, has been restored, robbing it of some of its antique flavour but the faces of the stucco Buddhas in the niches reflect the tranquil air of the original.

More impressive is the 10th-century hilltop **Wat Phra That Chom Kitti** down the same dirt road. At its base are the three broken *chedi* of Wat Chom Chang. Climb the moss-covered stairway to the 25-m (82-ft) *chedi*, covered in copper plates.

Return to the highway and re-enter the city walls of Chiang Saen. In ages past, the first impressive monument you would have seen is **Wat Chedi Luang**, a 58-m (190-ft) high octagonal *chedi* built in 1331 amidst teak trees. Next door is the **Chiang Saen Museum** (Wednesday to Sunday 9am–4pm) which houses a fine collection of Chiang Saen bronze Buddha images and other artefacts.

Wander through the back streets to find other *chedi* and ruins sitting next to wooden houses. There are some superb photographic opportunities here. Drive back to the river and turn right, exiting the town on H1129. At KM49, turn right and climb the hill on which **Wat Phra That Pha Ngao** is situated. Beside the rather ordinary *chedi* is a steel tower. Climb to the top for a magnificent view of the Mekong River and the Laotian countryside.

Wat Pasak, Chiang Saen

There are now two all-weather roads to the border settlement of **Chiang Khong**, some 53km (33 miles) away on the Mekong River. The lower route has good views of the river, whilst the other route goes near hilltribe villages. There is not much of interest in **Chiang Khong**, save for the illicit trading that goes on with Laos, and the 13th-century **Wat Luang** in the middle of the town. Accommodation in Chiang Khong is available at **Golden Resort**, a five-room, Thai-style house. Contact the housekeeper Khun Malika, tel: 791350, for reservations.

Return to Chiang Rai by bus or your rented car. From Chiang Rai, buses leave every hour for the 3½-hour journey to Chiang Mai. If you are driving, take H1020 and H1152 via Phaya Mengrai.

Morning view of the misty Mekong River delta

A week-long excursion to Pai, midway between Chiang Mai and Mae Hong Son and back. Highlights include a 2–3 day whitewater rafting trip down Pai River, a Shan village visit, and an excursion to Mae Sariang and Ob Luang Gorge on the return trip.

The streets of Pai

Orange bus No 612 departs from the Chiang Mai Arcade Bus Station (Platform 9) at two-hourly intervals from 7am to 2.30pm for the 135-km (84-mile) four-hour trip to Pai. If you are driving or riding a motorcycle, head north on H107 towards Mae Taeng (KM36), then turn left onto H1095. This journey down a country road (see map on page 52/53) is guaranteed to blow the city out of your pores. The drive is along a paved but twisted road that climbs ridges and threads valleys, and through superb mountain scenery studded with small hamlets. The road finally enters a broad valley and the small town of **Pai** which lies on the banks of the **Pai River** and has the air of an alpine village. Small hotels line the main street, including the facetiously named Pai in the Sky. Spend the day enjoying its peace.

Rent a bicycle near the bus station or walk to the base of the hill near **Wat Mae Yen** (Temple on the Hill) to the east. Continue past the temple to visit **Shan villages**, eventually intersecting with the main road. Just past the wooden bridge is a turn to the right that takes you along the river through three more Shan villages on a 4½-km (3-mile) loop that will bring you back to the highway and into Pai itself. The Shans, also known as Thai Yai (Great Thais) are believed to have migrated from China's Yunnan province, moving down rivers and streams into the upper valleys of the Southeast Asian river system in the 10th century. Many settled in Upper Burma while others went on to parts of Thailand such as Pai.

There are other walks and rides to the west of town. Head past the Pai Hospital on a 7-km (4¼-mile) journey that will take you past Shan and Lahu villages to end at a pretty waterfall. The road is better suited to feet than to bicycles but with perseverance you can make the ride.

If you happen to be in Pai between July and December each year, the Thai Adventure Co Ltd in Pai (tel: 699111, Guy Golias) operates interesting and exciting whitewater rafting trips ranging from two to three days down the Pai River through wild countryside. On the first day, you will be driven 64km (39¾ miles) to a branch of the Pai River, where you board rubber rafts and paddle past a wildlife sanctuary. Break for lunch and a swim. You will make another short afternoon trip before setting up camp, cooking dinner and settling down for the night.

The next day is a morning walk to the **Wind Cave**. After lunch, you will raft to the Pai River with its Class 2–3 rapids (Class 1 being the tamest and Class 6 the most difficult) and interesting hot springs. Camp overnight by a freshwater stream in the forest.

Day three takes you rafting again, this time through the **Pai Canyon** and four more rapids, ending at the Mae Hong Son valley at about 2pm, where lunch is served. From here, you will be transferred to Mae Hong Son.

This 50-km (31-mile) trip can be done in two days by omitting the walk to Wind Cave. The Thai Adventure Co Ltd is located at **Chez Swan Restaurant** on Pai's main street, Rungaiyanon Road. This restaurant is highly recommended for its French and Thai cuisine

If you would rather not raft, buses leave from Pai at 7, 9 and 11am, and 1.30pm for the 110-km (68-mile) journey to Mae

Whitewater rafting down the Pai River

Hong Son. The scenery is more rugged, with long narrow valleys and pine-topped ridges that look into deep valleys. Beyond Soppong the views towards Burma are breathtaking. The bus arrives in **Mae Hong Son** four hours later. For details of how to spend two days in the town, see *Excursion 11*.

From Mae Hong Son, it is 350km (217 miles) back to Chiang Mai by the southern route. Buses depart the station at 6 and 8am and 12.30, 8 and 9pm for the 8-hour journey through hills and narrow, rice-terraced valleys. Break your journey in **Mae Sariang**, four hours down the road. Mae Sariang offers fine views along its river and two temples, one behind the other. The first, **Wat Uttayarom**, is undistinguished, but the second, **Wat Boonruang**, has the multi-tiered roofs and wooden lacework one associates with east coast American shore homes built in the 1890s.

From Mae Sariang, the road heads due east. Along the way are several rest stops: look out for signs with a tree falling on a picnic table. At KM17 is **Ob Luang National Park** (Thailand's mini-version of the Grand Canyon), where a fast-flowing river pours through a narrow gap. H1088 rejoins H108 at **Hot**, little more than a wide spot in the road. The bus continues through **Chom Thong** with its lovely **Wat Phra That Si Chom Thong** (see *Excursion 8*) and brings you back to Chiang Mai.

Shopping

Antiques

Statues crafted from wood, bronze, terracotta, and stone are commonly found in Chiang Mai's antique shops as are carved wooden angels, mythical animals, temple bargeboards and eave brackets. Most Buddha images come from Burma as the Thai government has banned the export of these items. Bronze deer, angels, and characters from the *Ramakhien* cast in bronze do not fall under the export ban. If you are interested in their decorative value rather than their antiquity, then consider fake antiques. With genuine antiques in short supply, Thailand's artisans have turned to creating copies. There is no attempt to sell these as antique items and the craftsmanship is often quite remarkable. Images of deities, animals, children, betelnut boxes and a range of other goods in a variety of finishes are very popular.

Furniture

Wooden furniture in a variety of finishes, including a light whitewash and pastel colours, include cabinets, tables, dining room sets, bedroom sets or something as simple as a wooden tray or trivet. Chiang Mai artisans are known for their expertise in carving floral motifs and other intricate designs.

Basketware

Thailand makes some superb wicker and bamboo items but the ones found in Chiang Mai tend towards farm utensils. You can find lamps, storage boxes, tables, colourful mats, handbags, letter holders, tissue boxes and slippers in some of the larger emporia.

Fabrics and Clothes

More than any other craft, Thai silk is synonymous with Thailand. Sold in a wide variety of colours, its hallmark is the tiny nubs

Woodcraft products

An artisan applying laquer to a wooden horse

which, like embossings, rise from its shimmering surface. Unlike sheer Indian silks, the thick, iridescent Thai silk lends itself both to clothes and to use in furnishings for the house.

Thai silk is sold in plain or printed lengths or cut into scarves and other accessories. Tailors in Chiang Mai can fashion the silk into blouses and dresses but the quality of the cut and finish varies. If using a tailor, take along a magazine illustration or a ready-made dress, and allow time for more than one fitting.

Cotton is popular for shirts and dresses since it 'breathes' in the hot, humid air. Although available in lengths, it is generally tailored into dresses and shirts. In markets like Chang Khlan you can find cotton jackets made by the hilltribes, dark blue farmers' shirts and casual clothes.

Ceramics

Most Thai ceramics are produced in the North, the best known of which is celadon. The jade-green glaze of celadon coats statues, lamps, ashtrays and other items. Celadon is done in dark green, brown and cobalt blue hues.

Modelled after its Chinese cousin, blue-and-white porcelain includes pots, lamp bases, household items and figurines. The quality varies widely depending on the skill employed and the firing and glazing.

Bencharong, (five colour pottery) describes a style of fine porcelain derived from Chinese art in the 16th century. Normally reserved for bowls and containers, its classic pattern surrounds small religious figures with intricate floral designs. *Bencharong* is usually rendered in green, blue, yellow, rose and black.

Bencharong porcelain

Thai earthenware includes a wide assortment of pots, planters, and dinner sets in a rainbow of colours and designs.

Home Decorative Items

Burmese in origin and style, *kalaga* wall hangings depicting gods, kings and mythical animals have gained immense popularity in the past few years. The figures are stuffed with *kapok* to make them stand out from the surface in bas relief. Also popular are the artificial blooms made from fabric, plastic, polyester and paper, virtually indistinguishable from the fresh variety. Paper mâché crafted into animals, boxes and vases also make interesting gifts.

Gems and Jewellery

Thailand is a leading producer of rubies and sapphires. Rough-cut and polished stones are sold for a fraction of their cost overseas. Light green Burmese jade is carved into jewellery and art objects.

Be warned that there are unscrupulous dealers who pass off fakes as genuine and claim a gold content far in excess of the true value. Unless you know what you are doing, you can be cheated. Ask for a certificate of authenticity but be prepared even then to have difficulty retrieving your money if you later discover the gem to be a fake.

Costume jewellery is a major Thai craft with numerous items available. Especially popular are fresh orchids dipped in gold and crafted into earrings, brooches and necklaces.

Lacquerware

Lacquerware is a Lanna speciality and comes in two varieties: the gleaming gold and black type normally seen on the shutters of temple windows, and the matte red type with black and/or green details which originated in Northern Thailand and Burma.

The lacquerware range includes ornate containers and trays, wooden figurines, woven bamboo baskets and Burmese-inspired Buddhist manuscripts. The pieces may also be studded with tiny glass mosaics and gilded ornaments.

Hilltribe Crafts

The Hmong, Yao, Lisu, Lahu, Akha and Karen produce a wide variety of brightly-coloured needlepoint work in geometric and floral patterns. Panels of these needlepoint work are sewn onto shirts, coats, bags and other clothing items. Hilltribe silver work is valued less for its silver content (which is low) than for the intricate work that goes into making it. The selection includes necklaces, head-dresses, bracelets and rings the women wear on ceremonial occasions. Other items include knives, baskets, pipes and a gourd flute that looks and sounds like a bagpipe.

Hilltribe crafts

Leather

The items are prosaic enough – shoes, bags, wallets, attaché cases, belts – but the animals which have contributed their hides are the oddest assortment: snake, pangolin, cow, crocodile, lizard, frog and even chicken.

Metal Art Objects

Although Thai craftsmen have produced some of Asia's most beautiful Buddha images, modern bronze sculpture tends to be of less exalted subjects and execution. Minor deities, characters from the classical literary saga, the *Ramakhien*, deer and abstract figures are cast up to 2m (6ft) tall and are normally annealed with brass, making them gleam. Bronze is also cast into cutlery. Silverworking is an ancient Chiang Mai art. Jewellery, trays and other items are sold in the shops by the piece but in small home foundries are sold by weight. The craftsmanship can be extremely fine and the item can make a lasting gift.

Umbrellas

Chiang Mai's most famous product, Chiang Mai umbrellas, once made from silk and oiled paper, now comes in a wide variety of sizes and materials. What makes the unbrellas especially attractive are the nature-inspired motifs handpainted on them. No longer created simply to protect fair skins from the nasty sun, the umbrellas can be as large as 4m (13ft) in diameter, big enough to shade a patio table.

The materials used vary from cotton and silk to *sah* paper made from pounded mulberry tree bark, one of the oldest types of paper known. A related product is the huge silk fan, used as wall decorations, and lampshades. Prices range from 15 baht for tiny umbrellas to 4,000 baht for the big ones. You will find a whole variety at Borsang Village, east of Chiang Mai.

Where To Shop

The specialist shops along **Borsang Road** (see *Day 2*) produce particular types of crafts. There are several large emporia on the same road although the products carry slightly higher price tags.

For wood products, your best bet is the village of **Baan Tawai** (see *Excursion 7*) just south of Chiang Mai. The quality of carving and painting varies widely as do the types and finishes of items. Prices can be bargained and items can be shipped.

Operating under the patronage of King Bhumibol, the Hilltribe Products Foundation runs two shops. The main shop, **Border Crafts of Thailand**, is at 21/17 Suthep Road, Wat Suan Dok (tel: 277743) while the branch, **Hilltribe Products Foundation** (tel: 212978) is at 100/61-62 Huai Kaeo Road near Chiang Mai University. These shops, in a programme run by the Royal Family, aid hilltribes in preserving their traditions and skills by providing them with a market for their products.

Eating Out

As elsewhere in Thailand, one of the pleasures of a visit to Chiang Mai is the chance to dine on fine food. The dining options range from Thai, which is rapidly gaining popularity in the West, to Continental and Asian. Best of all, the prices are quite reasonable. An added attraction of eating out in Chiang Mai is the lovely settings of its restaurants: old Lanna homes, riverside inns and gardens ensure a different dining experience every evening.

A Taste of Thailand

Thai dishes are as individual and as varied as the chefs who prepare them. The cooks rely on garlic, lemon grass, chillies, coriander, fish paste and dozens of herbs and spices to impart an astounding variety of flavours to the dishes. Although most dishes are spicy, they can be made less fiery on request. Among the spicy favourites are *thom yam gung* (piquant soup with shrimp), *gaeng khiew wan gai* (a hot green curry with chicken or beef) and *gaeng phet* (a red curry with beef).

Non-spicy dishes include: *thom kha gai* (coconut milk curry with chicken), *plaamuk thawd krathiem prik thai* (squid or fish fried with garlic and black pepper), *nua phat namman hoi* (beef in oyster sauce) and *muu phat priew wan* (sweet and sour pork). In addition,

Thai desserts often contain coconut

Tossing som-dtam, a Thai-style salad

there is Chiang Mai's own cuisine whose key dishes are listed on the next page.

For a Thai-style breakfast, wander into the side streets by the **Ton Lamyai market**. Sidewalk vendors will be deep-frying the tasty X-shaped pastries called *patongkoh*. Order them with the very thick but tasty Thai coffee served with a layer of condensed milk at the bottom. Insist on Cafe Thai or you will be served Nescafe which, while delicious, lacks the punch of the Thai variety.

Desserts

Desserts are invariably sweet. Try coconut ice cream (ice cream *kathit*) and a host of sweets with a base of coconut milk and incorporating sticky rice and luscious fruits. The traditional Thai meal-ender is a plate of fresh fruit, usually papaya, pineapple and watermelon, peeled and cut into bite-sized chunks. Vary it with banana, tangerine and seasonal fruits like jackfruit, rambutan, mangoes and mangosteen. If you crave a taste treat akin to a gourmet Limburger cheese, bite into a durian.

Drinks

For a refreshing drink, try a shake made of pureed fruit, crushed ice and a light syrup. Chilled young coconuts are delicious: drink the juice, then scrape out and eat the tender young flesh. Soft drinks like Coca-Cola are found everywhere. Try Vitamilk, a refreshing drink made from soybeans. For a revitalising cooler, order a bottle of soda, a glass of ice and a sliced lime. Squeeze the lime

Northern Cuisine

Khao Niew. Northern food is generally eaten with *khao niew* or sticky rice. One kneads a bit of rice into a ball and dips it in various sauces and curries.

Sai Oua. A chewy, oily, spicy pork sausage also called *nam* and associated with the North. It is roasted over a fire fuelled by coconut husks which impart a delicious aroma to the meat. Although normally prepared hygienically, it is best to buy *sai oua* only at better restaurants. Hot *prik kii nuu* chillies buried inside the sausages present the unwary with a painful surprise.

Khao Soy. Originally a Burmese speciality, this delicious egg noodle dish is filled with chunks of beef or chicken, and served lightly curried in a gravy of coconut cream. A sprinkle of crispy noodles and chopped garlic goes on top.

Nam Prik Ong. Minced pork, chillies, tomatoes, garlic and shrimp paste are blended and chilled. It is served with crisp cucumber slices, parboiled cabbage leaves and crispy pork rind (the latter is another Northern snack).

Northern roast chicken

Larb. A minced pork, chicken, beef, or even fish, dish. *Larb* is associated with Northeastern cuisine where it is thoroughly cooked. *Larb* in the North, however, is normally eaten raw. It is served with long beans, mint leaves, cabbage, and other raw vegetables which contrast with its full-bodied meaty flavour.

Gaeng Hang Lay. Originally from Burma, it is one of the Northern dishes. Those with tender palates should approach this dish with some caution. Tamarind imparts to this pork curry a somewhat sweet and sour flavour. The curry is especially suitable as a dip for balls of sticky rice.

Mieng is a Burmese delicacy of fermented tea leaves that tastes a lot better than it sounds.

Khantoke. This buffet of northern dishes provides an excellent introduction to Northern cuisine. Lest you think it is served only to tourists, wander through a morning market and see steaming pots of its key dishes set out for customers. A typical Khantoke dinner includes five main dishes: *gaeng hang lay* (pork curry with garlic and ginger), *nam prik ong* (minced pork with tomato and chilli paste), *khaeb muu* (pork crackling), *larb* (minced pork, chicken, fish or beef); and *sai oua* (spicy northern pork sausage).

Deep-fried patongkoh sticks

into the glass, add the soda and, voila, your thirst is slaked. Coffee drinkers will enjoy the very strong Thai coffee bolstered with chicory or tamarind. The odd orange-coloured Thai tea is sticky sweet but delicious. On a hot day, the Chinese drink a glass of hot, very thin tea, as they believe that ice is bad for the stomach, but all three drinks taste great over ice.

Local beers include Singha, Chang and Kloster. The best local whisky since 1939 is called Mekhong, distilled from glutinous rice and usually bought by the half-bottle. It is best drunk with plenty of soda, ice and – very importantly – a squeeze of lime. Most foreign liquors are available, and the better Western restaurants normally have wine lists.

Restaurants

Eating out in Chiang Mai generally costs much less than Bangkok and other tourist centres like Phuket and Koh Samui. The approximate cost of a meal for one person, without drinks, is categorised as follows: $ = less than 50 baht; $$ = 50–100 baht; $$$ = 100–250 baht; $$$$ = over 250 baht.

Thai

Antique House ($$$) at 71 Charoen Prathet Road serves Thai food in a beautiful, old house. Recommended dishes here include its delectable steamed chicken which is prepared Chiang Mai-style, as well as the various spicy salads. From 7pm there are traditional dancing shows.

Have breakfast in a garden restaurant

Krua Khun Phan ($$$) is at 80/1 Inthawarorot Road (near Suan Dok Gate), tel: 214557. It is one of several Thai restaurants that are behind Wat Phra Singh. The restaurant's appeal lies in its displays of ready-made Thai dishes and in the homely atmosphere of its dining hall.

The Smiling Monkey ($$$), 40/1 Bumrungburi Road, tel: 277538, is a pretty garden restaurant in the old city, right next to the southern moat. Good Central and Northern Thai food. This is also an ideal location for a quiet drink; at the back of the restaurant is a friendly little bar. Open daily 11am–2pm and 4pm–2am.

Diamond Riverside Hotel ($$$) on Charoen Prathet Road serves a Lanna *khantoke* dinner at 7pm followed by classical Lanna and hilltribe dancing. This is a good way of combining Northern Thai cuisine with Lanna culture. Call 270080 for reservations.

Chiang Mai Cultural Centre ($$$) at 185/3 Wua Lai Road offers a similar programme with a *khantoke*-style dinner beginning at 7pm followed by a cultural show in a large hall and a hilltribe presentation outside. The dinner show ends at about 10pm. Call 275097 for reservations.

Khrua Sabai ($$), at the golf driving range opposite Airport Plaza, tel: 274042 has Thai-Chinese food that is highly recommended.

Aroon-Rai ($$) at 46 Kotchasan Road (tel: 276947) has been around for decades. Ambassadors and ministers of state have had meals here, praising its tasty Thai and Northern Thai dishes. The staff are friendly, and used to helping English-speaking visitors find their way around the menu.

Riverside Restaurant ($$) at 9–11 Charoen Rat Road opposite Chinda Hospital, tel: 243239, has been for some years a popular meeting place for visitors. If you are looking for a quiet dinner, go elsewhere. If you want a cheerful, convivial atmosphere this is it. Overlooking the Ping River, it serves excellent meals and offers a host of live bands playing middle-of-the-road classics.

Kai Wan ($$$) at 181 Soi 9, Nimmanhamin Road, tel: 222147, is a wooden Thai house set in a pleasant garden. Lunch is served in an open-sided room under the house, dinner on the balcony upstairs. Popular with residents as well as visitors.

Grilled Chicken with Honey ($$) is both the name and the primary dish in this unpretentious restaurant, tel: 221364, on Charoen Prathet Road next to Pornping Hotel. It serves Northeastern food with *larb* (a raw vegetable salad with minced meat) and other favourites.

Vegetarian

Whole Earth ($$$), 88 Sri Dornchai Road, tel: 282463. Serves both Thai vegetarian and non-vegetarian dishes in a beautiful garden setting. Recommended dishes are *aloo gobi* (a cauliflower and potato Indian-

Relaxing at The Gallery

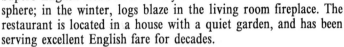

Riverside dining

style dry curry), Vietnamese spring rolls, and Thai curry with tofu and eggplant in coconut milk.

International

Daret's ($) at 4/5 Chaiyaphum Road, tel: 225440, is an outdoor restaurant where budget travellers gather. Despite the low prices, the food is quite good. Try Chicken Cordon Bleu and the fruit shakes. Come here if you crave a good banana split, to meet and watch people.

English

The Pub ($$$), 189 Huai Kaeo Road near the Amari Rincome Hotel, tel: 211550. Superb English meals in a homely atmosphere; in the winter, logs blaze in the living room fireplace. The restaurant is located in a house with a quiet garden, and has been serving excellent English fare for decades.

French

Le Coq d'Or ($$$$), 68/1 Koh Klang, Nong Hoi, tel: 282024. Established for over 20 years, this French restaurant is a favourite of Thai, foreign dignitaries and 'people who matter'. It's located in an old house and a bit inconvenient to get to but worth a try.

German

Bier Stube ($$), 33/6A Moon Muang Road, tel: 278869. Near Tha Pae Gate. Good, standard German fare.

Italian

Babylon ($$$), 100/63 Huai Kaeo Road, opposite the entrance to Chiang Mai University, tel: 212180. Specialises in pizza and a variety of Italian dishes. Open 11am–2pm, 6–10pm.

Japanese

Miyuki ($$$), Royal Princess Hotel, 112 Chang Khlan Road, tel: 281033. A restaurant much favoured by Japanese food aficionados.

Market Munching

For the adventurous, the delicious Thai fare at market and street stalls offer a new culinary experience. At the **Anusarn Market**, across from the Royal Princess Hotel on Chang Khlan Road to Charoen Prathet Road, are stalls with names like **Number One Cock Fire**, and **Fatty Fatty**, each specialising in a different dish. Among the many possibilities are honey roasted chicken, *guay tiew phat Thai* (fried noodles with shrimp, pork and bean sprouts), and *khai jiew hoy* (eggs scrambled with a generous serving of mussels).

77

Nightlife

Nightlife in Chiang Mai was inconceivable some 30 years ago. All the same, the Blue Moon started business in a subdued way and is still in business with a lively band and an array of singers. For those who enjoy dancing, the larger hotels have discos. Alongside the moat, near Tha Phae Gate, are a variety of bars, some with live bands, taped music and videos, others with music and hostesses. Taking their cue from Bangkok, some Patpong-style bars have opened with go-go girls.

Still, nightlife in Chiang Mai is subdued compared with that of Bangkok. Perhaps, it is the fatigue induced by trekking or the calmer feeling and more restful nature of the North. For many visitors to Chiang Mai, nightlife is shopping or eating out at the night markets in Chang Khlan Road.

Music Bars

Among the most popular are **Western Art** on Sri Phum Road, with live music every night, and **Touch** on Huai Kaew Road. At the **Cottage and Decor**, 27 Chiang Mai-Lamphun Road, a band plays jazz nightly. Country and western is not forgotten in this neck of the woods at the **West Side Pub** on Singkham Road. Thai folk music is occasionally thrown in for good measure. If livewire bars are not your scene, the intimate **Blues Pub** at 33/6 Moon Muang Road will go down well. For a deliciously different Thai experience, go to **Sethee** at 8/23 Bunruangrit Road and be entertained by a

Friendly bar hostesses

troupe of Thai singers decked up in bizarre costumes. The audience and performers seem to enjoy it, and occasionally a comedy team from Bangkok will take the stage.

Hostess Bars

Blue Moon, 5/3 Moon Muang Road is a typical large Thai-style nightclub with attractive hostesses. Worth a visit, if you don't fancy sitting all by yourself.

Gay Bars

Kra Jiap Pub at 18/1 Soi 3 Wua Lai Road is open from 11–2am. There is also a nightly cabaret show at 10pm. **The Coffee Boy** at 248 Thung Hotel Road is housed in an old Thai Lanna teak house. Patrons enjoy classical music in a peaceful setting. Be forewarned, though, that this bar is located in a seedy side of town. Open 8pm–2am; with special shows on Friday, Saturday and Sunday, from 11pm.

Massages

Traditional massages are offered at the following places: **Diamond Riverside Hotel**, 33/10 Chareon Prathet Road, tel: 270081; **Northern Blind School** at the corner of Arak Street and Soi 1, Inthawarorot Road near Suan Dok Gate, tel: 221009; and **Rinkaew Phovech**, 183/4 Wua Lai Road, beside the Old Chiang Mai Cultural Centre, tel: 274565. Daily 8am–8pm. For a more risque body massage, head for the **Saiyuri** at Soi 2, Bamrungrat Road, tel: 242361.

Cinemas

Vista Hotel, near the railway station, has two cinemas, **Vista One** and **Vista Two**. There is also another **Vista Cinema** at the Central Department Store Complex on Huai Kaeo Road. **Mahanakorn Theatre** near the Chang Pheuak Gate on the highway north shows Thai movies that run the gamut from tragedy to comedy, all within 100 or so minutes. That the films are in Thai should not deter you: there is enough dramatics in Thai films to convey their meaning for the non-Thai speaker.

Discos

Among the city's more popular dancing spots are **Bubbles** at the Pornping Hotel on Charoen Prathet Road, **The Wall** at Chiang Inn Hotel along Chang Khlan Road and the **Biosphere Spacedrome** at Charoen Muang Road. Competing for the crowds is **Touch** at 36/9 Huai Kaew Road. Open from 5pm till the early hours of the morning, this is a lively venue. With two floors and good live music this is a place to see and be seen.

For something really zany, head for the **Climax** at Osathapan Road. You can expect to see people dancing around a table covered with tasty snacks, a Thai phenomenon known as *khrua tech*, or kitchen disco.

Calendar of Special Events

Thais celebrate their religious holidays with verve and invite the visitor to join in. As dates change, you should check with the Tourism Authority of Thailand (TAT) office first.

A radiant Miss Borsang finalist

JANUARY

Borsang Umbrella Fair: This colourful festival honours the craftsmen of one of the oldest of Chiang Mai arts – umbrellas. There are competitions and exhibitions, and the highlight of the fair is a beauty pageant where the annual Miss Borsang is selected.

FEBRUARY

Luang Wiang Lakhon: Lampang's five most important Buddha images are paraded through the streets. Nightly Sound and Light presentations take place at the historic Wat Phra That Lampang Luang.

Flower Festival: Held when Chiang Mai's flowers are abloom. Flower exhibitions are staged but the key event is a grand floral procession through the streets of the city, with floats, marching bands and beautiful Chiang Mai women.

Magha Puja: Celebrates the spontaneous gathering of 1,250 disciples to hear Buddha preach. As the full moon rises, Buddhists gather at temples. Join in by buying incense sticks, a candle and flowers from a vendor. After the chanting, follow the monkled procession around the temple. After three circuits, place your candle, incense sticks and flowers in the sand-filled trays as others are doing, make a *wai* (hands clasped before the face) and depart.

APRIL

Poy Sang Long (Mae Hong Son and Chiang Mai): Young Shan men are initiated into the Buddhist monkhood in this ceremony.

Songkran: The traditional Thai New Year finds the Thais at their boisterous best. One is supposed to bless friends by sprinkling water on them, but it soon gets out of hand and water flies everywhere. Expect to get drenched and dress accordingly. The main action takes place on the banks of the Ping River.

MAY

Visakha Puja: Commemorates the Buddha's birth, enlightenment and death, all of which occurred on the

Floral float at the Krathong festival

same day. Celebrated in the same manner as Magha Puja except that Chiang Mai residents walk up Doi Suthep to make merit.

Lychee Fair: Chiang Rai's lychee harvest is the reason for the celebration. The Lychee Fair features displays of agricultural products and handicrafts and a beauty contest to select a Miss Lychee.

Intakin Festival: Held at Chiang Mai's Wat Chedi Luang for seven days and nights to invoke blessings for the city and its inhabitants.

JULY

Asalaha Puja: Commemorates Buddha's first sermon to his first five disciples. It is celebrated in the same manner as Magha and Vishaka Puja.

AUGUST

Longan Fair: Like Chiang Rai's Lychee Fair, Lamphun's Longan Fair celebrates the harvest of the *lamyai* fruit, for which the town is best known. Among the key events is the selection of a Miss Lamyai, who joins the ranks of other Northern beauty queens like (no kidding!) Miss Garlic and Miss Onion.

SEPTEMBER

Chinese Moon Festival: Celebrated on the full moon night of the eighth lunar month. Do not miss the lanterns and the luscious pastry moon cakes filled with sweet bean paste, durian and salted eggs.

NOVEMBER

Yi Peng Loy Krathong: Loy Krathong is the most beautiful of Thai celebrations. As the full moon rises, Thais fill tiny floral boats with candles and incense and launch them into the rivers, canals, ponds, and the sea to wash away sins and bless love affairs. It is a romantic night for lovers of all ages. Buy a *krathong* from a vendor, light the taper and incense, place in it a small coin and a few hairs plucked from your head, say a prayer and send it on its way down the Ping River. At nightfall there is a procession of colourful decorated floats down Tha Phae Road and past the Municipal offices. In recent years this festival has been ruined by the excessive use of firecrackers. Take care of yourself – and of small children.

Sunflower Fair (Mae Hong Son only): The Mexican sunflowers are in bloom during this time in the hills near Doi Mae U-Khor. Mae Hong Son organises a three-day festival. Highlights are oxcarts decorated with the beautiful flowers, cultural exhibitions, a beauty contest, film shows, music and a Thai Yai folk drama.

Buddhist Temple Fairs: During the cool season from November through February, temple fairs are held to raise money for temple repairs. In the evening, villagers gather to enjoy local drama troupes, carnival rides, and booths selling farm products. There is a convivial air of good fun all over Chiang Mai.

DECEMBER

Chiang Mai Winter Fair: The annual winter fair, held at the Municipal Stadium in Chiang Mai, offers cultural shows, the Miss Chiang Mai contest and a product fair.

Practical Information

GETTING THERE

By Air

Thai Airways operates several daily flights between Chiang Mai and Bangkok (60 minutes). Chiang Mai is also connected by air with Chiang Rai, Mae Hong Son, Nan, Mae Sot, Phitsanuloke, Khon Kaen and Phuket. Check details with the local Thai Airways office as flight schedules may change. Some flights may have Business Class seats at extra cost.

Note that the four daily flights to and from Chiang Mai and Mae Hong Son are susceptible to cancellation because of mist, rain or low cloud cover. Take this into account when planning your trip.

There are also international flights between Chiang Mai and Singapore, Hong Kong, Burma (Myanmar) and Laos.

From the airport: Situated at the southwest corner of the town, Chiang Mai Airport is a 10-minute drive from the city centre. Mini-buses from major hotels ferry guests with reservations (one can make bookings at the airport) to their premises.

Thai Airways also operates a limousine service to all hotels and a shuttle bus service to the Thai Airways office in town.

Airport tax: The airport tax for passengers departing to other domestic destinations is 30 baht. For international flights, the airport tax is 500 baht tax.

By Rail

Each day, several train services run between Bangkok and Chiang Mai, covering a distance of 751km (467 miles). The day train journey takes 13 hours and requires lots of stamina but it is more fun than flying.

Day trains leave Bangkok's Hualampong Station daily at 6.40am and arrive in Chiang Mai at 7.35pm. The return trip leaves at 6.35am and arrives in Bangkok at 7.50pm.

In addition, there are four overnight sleeper trains which leave Bangkok at 3pm, 6pm, 7.40pm – the Nakhon Ping Express – and 10pm daily, arriving in Chiang Mai at 5am, 7.10am, 7.55am and 11.30am respectively. Return trains leave Chiang Mai at 3.30pm, 4.40pm, 8.40pm and 9.05pm – the Nakhon Ping Express – arriving in Bangkok at 5.25am, 6am, 10.25am and 9.40am respectively.

The sit-up only Sprinter train leaves Bangkok's Hualampong Station at 8.10am and arrives in Chiang Mai at 6.50pm, almost 11 hours later. The Sprinter departs Chiang Mai at 7.40pm and arrives at Bangkok at 6.15am the next morning.

The evening train departures from Bangkok give you enough hours of light the next morning to enjoy the climb to the 1½-km (1-mile) tunnel through the

Khun Tan Hills. The station just beyond the tunnel is the highest point on the Royal Thai Railway system, at 578m (1,900ft). Then, the train descends and travels through rice fields and orchards until it reaches the terminus.

Both the First and Second Class air-conditioned coaches are comfortable, and

Bangkok–Chiang Mai day train

sleepers are available on these services. Food on the trains is not a problem as there is a restaurant car, and food vendors on board or at the station platforms.

The trains can be very full at times and it is advisable to make advance reservations. Make your bookings at Bangkok's Hualampong Station or the Chiang Mai Railway Station.

TRAVEL ESSENTIALS

When to Visit

Chiang Mai's best months are mid-November through mid-February when the air is cool and the skies are clear. From February through May, the sun shines and it is hot and dry. The monsoon rain (June through mid-November) falls sporadically so that a visit can be pleasant albeit under frequently overcast skies.

During the Christmas and New Year holidays and the week of Chinese New Year facilities are strained to breaking point; book well in advance.

Visas and Passports

Visitors from most countries, including the UK and the US, are issued 2- or 4-week entry permits on arrival and upon presentation of a passport and a ticket for the return or onward journey. Visitors from Korea, Denmark, Finland, New Zealand, Norway and Sweden only are issued a 90-day entry permit. Entry per-

mits cannot be extended while you are in Thailand. It is advisable to check with a Thai embassy or consulate in your country before departure.

If you are planning a longer stay, apply for either a 60-day tourist visa or 30-day transit visa from Thai embassies and consulates overseas. These can be extended at the Chiang Mai branch of the Immigration Division (tel: 277510; open Monday to Friday, from 8.30am–12pm and 1–4.30pm) at Fang Road, just before entering Chiang Mai Airport.

Visitors who wish to leave Thailand and return before the expiration of their visas can apply for a re-entry permit prior to their departure at the Immigration Division in Chiang Mai. Note: an exit visa is not required.

The Immigration Division enforces a strict dress code. Dress neatly and decently as visitors who are not wearing 'polite clothes' will not be served.

Customs

The import of drugs, dangerous chemicals, pornography, firearms and ammunition is banned. Smuggling heroin and other hard drugs is an offence punishable by death. Foreigners are allowed to bring in without tax, one camera with five rolls of film, 200 cigarettes and one litre wine or spirits. There are no limits on the amount of foreign currency a visitor can bring in. On leaving, the maximum amount of Thai currency that can be taken out without authorisation is 50,000 baht.

Vaccinations

Although the threat from cholera, polio and typhoid is minimal and inoculations are no longer required for entry into Thailand, vaccinations are recommended. Injections against Hepatitis A and B are advised. Smallpox is no longer a threat. Yellow fever inoculation is essential if you are coming from an infected area.

Climate

The North's popularity stems in part from its pleasant climate. Temperatures from mid-November to January average between 13°C and 28°C (56°F–83°F) in Chiang Mai; the hills are even cooler.

Temperatures begin rising in February and in the hot season (March–May) range between 17°C and 36°C (63°–97°F). In the rainy season (June–mid-November) the highs drop marginally but the lows, not at all. There is no considerable variation between day and night-time temperatures in any season.

The monsoon in the North begins (May) and ends (October) earlier than in Central Thailand. Overcast skies predominate but the rain generally falls sporadically except during September when an average of 250 mm (10 inches) crashes down and city streets often flood.

Clothing

Natural fibres and blends are preferred because they breathe well in moist air. Cool season evenings can be quite chilly (the record low for Chiang Rai is 2°C (35°F). If trekking in the hills, it can be even colder. A sweater or jacket will be welcome in the evenings or when travelling by bike. Wear several layers of clothing that can be peeled off as the day warms.

Shorts and sleeveless blouses for men and women are frowned upon at Buddhist temples. Because shoes must be removed upon entering a temple, it is more convenient to wear sandals or slip-ons. Wear a sturdy pair of leather shoes or running shoes if you plan to motorcycle. A hat is advisable on a hot day as are sunglasses.

The winter months in Chiang Mai are surprisingly dry, so moisturising lotion and chapstick will be welcome.

Electricity

Electric current runs at 220 volts, 50 cycles. Electrical outlets take only flat-pronged plugs only so bring a converter.

Time Differences

Chiang Mai is 7 hours ahead of GMT.

GETTING ACQUAINTED

Geography

Thailand is generally divided into four regions, each of them capitalised, eg, North, as in North, South, East, and West. The 'North' refers to the entire northern region which surrounds Chiang Mai. Non-capitalised 'north' refers to directions, for eg, 'northeast'.

The North lies between Laos in the east and the Tanen Taunggyi mountain range forming the Burmese border in the west; and between Burma and the Mekong River in the north and the upper rim of the Chao Phraya River Valley in the south. It is a hilly region with mountain ranges running north and south and the towns occupying the valleys. In the North, Thailand's highest mountain, Doi Inthanon, towers 2,565m (8,400ft) above the surrounding hills.

Chiang Mai, some 600km (373 miles) north of Bangkok, is the political and geographic capital of the North by virtue of its central position and size. As Thailand's second largest city, it is home to some 200,000 people and dominates the economic and social life of the Chiang Mai Valley. The valley is drained by the Ping River, one of four main tributaries which rise in the North and flow south to become the Chao Phraya, the country's most important river.

Outside the valley wall are five key regions of the North. To the west is the area comprising the valleys of Mae Chaem, Pai, Mae Hong Son and Mae Sarieng.

Beyond the Khun Tan range of mountains to the south is Lampang. The third area, to the east, encompasses cities like Phayao and Ngao. In the green valleys north of Chiang Mai are the Chiang Dao and Fang regions.

The fifth region is dominated by Chiang Rai. It is defined in the north and west by the Mekong River, an area known as the Golden Triangle for the three countries – Thailand, Burma and Laos – that border it and for its association with opium cultivation. Towns here include Mae Sai, Chiang Saen and Chiang Khong.

Two types of people inhabit the region: the Thais who are dominant, and a dozen hilltribes who are rice and vegetable farmers. (see also *History & Culture* chapter).

Government and Economy

Thailand is a constitutional monarchy with power vested in a freely-elected parliament and a senate appointed by His Majesty the King from civilian and mili-

A Chiang Mai lass

tary officials. The executive branch comprises a coalition of political parties which select a prime minister who in turn rules through a cabinet. There is also an independent judiciary.

Thailand enjoys a free-enterprise economy. Country-wide, tourism is the principal foreign exchange earner, followed by argicultural produce and commodities. In the North, prosperity has traditionally been based upon rice. Early in this century, teak logging became a major industry. After the lapse of the foreign company leases the supply of trees began to dwindle and logging was banned in 1989, although it still continues illegally.

In the 1970s, King Bhumibol introduced a host of new crops to the North. Today, brussels sprouts, strawberries, cantaloupes, mushrooms and a dozen other crops are grown. Coffee and tea plantations are plentiful, as are orchards of apples, peaches and other fruits normally associated with temperate climes.

Industry is being introduced primarily in the southern portion of Chiang Mai Valley and there is an air of prosperity about the larger towns with their new buildings and condominiums under construction. Unfortunately, much of the construction is dictated by economic considerations, with the result that the architectural integrity of its Lanna origins has been seriously compromised.

How Not to Offend

Thais regard the Royal Family with genuine reverence. Avoid making slighting remarks about royalty and always stand when the Royal Anthem is played before a movie.

Agriculture is the backbone of the North

Show similar respect to Buddha images, temples and monks. Thais take a dim view of men or women wearing shorts and sleeveless dresses when visiting temples. Thais are too polite to tell off a sloppy foreigner so the obligation is upon you to respect their religion as you would your own. Remove your shoes when you enter a Buddhist temple or a Taoist shrine.

A monk's vow of chastity prohibits him from touching a woman, even his mother. Women should stay clear of monks to avoid accidentally brushing against them.

The Thai greeting and farewell is *Sawasdee*. It is uttered while raising the hands in a prayer-like gesture, the fingertips touching the nose, and the upper portion of the body slightly bowed forward. This gesture is called the *wai*. It is easy to master and will earn you smiles aplenty.

Thais believe in personal cleanliness. Even those dressed in poor clothes are neat and clean. They frown on unkempt and unbathed foreigners and may refuse them service or treat them with less kindness than if properly attired.

Thais believe that the head is the fount of wisdom and all parts of the body from there down are progressively unclean. It is, therefore, an insult to touch another person on the head, point one's foot at him, or step over him. Kicking in anger is worse than spitting at him.

Hilltribe Etiquette

Hilltribes are animists and maintain a separate room in their houses for bones and other spirit objects. Some very good rules are offered by John R. Davies in his book *A Trekker's Guide to the Hilltribes of Northern Thailand.* Consider buying a copy of

you intend to visit the hilltribe villages. The following are some of the more salient points from Davies' book:

You should take photographs only after asking permission.

Do not touch the altar or attempt to sleep under or near it.

A star-shaped bamboo sign, that is normally placed above the main door, means that permission should be asked before entering the dwelling.

Davies also suggests observing these tribal rules:

Karens receive foreigners only on the verandah. It is taboo to touch tree stumps or burnt trees in the swidden areas.

Chiang Mai countryside

Enter a Hmong home only if invited by a male inhabitant; only if there are none around, then the woman of the house can admit you.

Avoid touching or leaning against the stove in a Yao house lest you offend the spirits that reside in it. Do not touch the sacred posts around a Lahu temple as they are a source of blessing.

Never touch the house posts or the entrance gates to Akha villages. Accept any offer to enter a house and take any refreshment offered to you. Men should not enter the women's sections of the houses.

Outsiders may not enter the bedrooms, touch the altar or sleep with their heads pointing towards the fire in a Lisu house. Foreign men and women cannot sleep together as they are usually placed in the guest room which also holds the family altar; the male should sleep in the main room. Never ever stand in the doorway with your feet on either side of it, and you should avoid stepping directly on the raised threshold.

Currency

The Thai baht is divided into 100 satangs. Bank note denominations include: 1,000 (light green), 500 (purple), 100 (red), 50 (blue), 20 (green) and 10 (brown) baht.

There are ten-baht coins (a brass coin encircled by a brass rim), five-baht coins (silver with copper rims), one-baht coins (silver) and two types of 50 and 25 satang coins (both brass-coloured).

The once stable Thai currency has been hit hard by Southeast Asia's economic problems. At press time it was rated at 40 baht to one US dollar. For current rates, check the *Bangkok Post* or *The Nation* newspapers.

Changing Money

There is no currency black market. Rates are more favourable for traveller's checks than for cash. Hotels generally give poor rates, so change money at a bank.

Banks are open from 8.30am–3.30pm daily except Saturday, Sunday and bank holidays (when they could be closed for four days in a row). Banks also operate exchange kiosks all over Chiang Mai.

Credit cards

Visa and Mastercard are accepted at most hotels, restaurants and big shops. Amex cards are less welcome because of their higher commission rate. You can also use credit cards to get cash advances at any of these banks: Bank of Ayudhaya, Thai Farmers Bank, Siam Commercial Bank and Thai Military Bank, Bangkok Bank, Krung Thai Bank (see page 98–99).

Tipping

Tipping is a new custom in Thailand, confined so far to large hotels and restaurants. Although a 10 percent service charge is added to the bill it usually goes to the owners so a small token to the waiter will

be appreciated. In ordinary restaurants, tip no more than 10 percent. There is no tipping in noodle shops or street stalls. Room boys can be tipped but will not expect it. Transport drivers are not tipped.

GETTING AROUND

Car Hire

Cars and jeeps can be rented at several locations. You need a valid international driver's license or one from your home state. As you have to surrender your passport for the duration of the rental period, change money first.

Rates begin at 800 baht per day and mileage is unlimited: you pay for the petrol you use. For example, Avis rents a Toyota Corona 1600 cc or Toyota Corolla 1300 cc/16 Valve for about 1,300–1,500 baht per day.

If you rent the car in Chiang Mai and leave it in Bangkok or another city with a Hertz or Avis office, you must pay a drop-off fee of 2,500 baht.

When renting, read the fine print carefully and be aware that you are liable for any damage to the vehicle. Ask for a comprehensive insurance which covers you and other vehicles involved in a collision.

Alternatively, hire a car with a driver to take you around Chiang Mai.

Avis: Main office, 14/14 Huai Kaeo Road (tel: 222013, 221316). Open 8am–5pm. Branches, Airport (tel: 270-222) and Royal Princess Hotel (tel: 281033/034).

Hertz: Main office, 90 Sri Dornchai Road (tel: 270184/87). Branches, Chiang Mai Plaza Hotel (tel: 279474) and Empress Hotel (tel: 270240).

Queen Bee Car Rent: 5 Moon Muang Road (tel: 275525).

Aod Car Rent: 49 Chang Khlan Road, opposite the night market (tel: 279220). Suzuki jeeps, cars, mini-buses with or without driver. Rentals rates are lower, with cars from 500 baht and jeeps from 1,500 baht per day including insurance and unlimited mileage.

Motorcycle Hire

You must surrender your passport for the duration of the rental period so change

money first. A photocopy may be accepted if you pay a deposit.

Motorcycles in Chiang Mai range from small 90 cc. Honda Dreams to 125 c.c. and 250 c.c. Honda, Suzuki and Yamaha trailbikes which have sufficient power to climb the North's hills. Rental companies can be found along Chang Khlan Road, Tha Phae Gate, and Chaiyaphum Road.

Prices range from 150–500 baht/day. Rental is for a 24-hour period and you may be able to bargain the price down if you rent for several days.

Tuk-tuks, Samlors and Songthaews

Tuk-tuks are motorised three-wheeled taxis, so-named for the noise they make when travelling. Charges are according to distance and start at 10–30 baht. Bargain for lower rates before you board.

Samlors, the pedal trishaws, charge 10 baht for short distances. As with *tuk tuks*, bargain before you board.

Songthaews are converted pick-ups with wooden benches on either side. Travelling on regular routes with other passengers costs 5–10 baht. Expect to pay more if

The Chiang Mai yellow bus

you travel off the regular routes.

You can bargain with *tuk-tuk* and *songthaew* drivers to take you just about anywhere in Chiang Mai and its environs. Expect to pay about 600 baht for an eight- or nine-hour day. The driver will wait for you at each site.

The drivers often make suggestions on places to visit. Avoid those offering to

take you shopping as they will very likely collect a hefty commission from the shops they take you to.

Bicycles

Shops along Chaiyaphum Road near Tha Phae Gate rent bicycles for 30 baht per day. Guesthouses like the Galare Guest House also rent bicycles.

HOURS & HOLIDAYS

Business Hours

Banks are open daily from 8.30am to 3.30pm except Saturday, Sunday and bank holidays. Currency exchange kiosks are open 8.30am–8.30pm. Post offices are open Monday to Friday from 8.30am to 4.30pm. In addition, all post offices are open on Saturday from 9am to 12pm. The Airport Post Office is open every day of the year from 8.30am–8pm. Businesses are open the usual office hours, except for hairdressers and barbers which tend to close on Wednesday. Shops are usually open from 9am–9pm daily.

Public Holidays

The following days are observed as official public holidays in Chiang Mai. The dates for many festivals change annually so make sure you check with the local Tourism of Thailand office.
New Year's Day: 1 January
Magha Puja: February/March

Chakri Memorial Day: 6 April
Songkran: 13 April
Labour Day: 1 May
Coronation Day: 5 May
Ploughing Ceremony: May
Visakha Puja: May/June
Asalaha Puja: July/August
HM the Queen's Birthday: 12 August
Chulalongkorn Day: 23 October
HM the King's Birthday: 5 December
Constitution Day: 10 December
New Year's Eve: 31 December
Chinese New Year: January/ February Although not officially recognised as a holiday, many shops are closed, often for several days.

ACCOMMODATION

Hotels

The following is a selection of hotels from among the many available in the North. A value added tax (VAT) of 10 percent and a service charge at 10 percent or more is added to the room rate.

The rate for a double room during the high season is categorised according to the following price ranges (taxes included):

$	=	less than 500 baht
$$	=	500–1,000 baht
$$$	=	1,000–2,000 baht
$$$$	=	over 2,000 baht

During peak holiday periods (holidays, Christmas, New Year, etc), rates go up significantly. But for the rest of the year, it is always worth asking for a discount.

If you are calling the hotel from outside North Thailand, please note that the telephone area code is 053.

Chiang Mai

(see also Mae Rim)

CHIANG MAI ORCHID
23 Huai Kaeo Road
Tel: 222091/99; Fax: 221625
267 rooms. Chiang Mai's top hotel, excellent facilities including fitness centre and pool. Extensive wine list. $$$$

CHIANG MAI PLAZA
92 Sri Dornchai Road
Tel: 270036/50; Fax: 272230
444 rooms. Centrally located in down-

Songthaews are economical

Tuk tuk travel

town Chiang Mai, with a coffee shop, and lobby bar with live music. Not far from the banks of the Ping River. $$$$

ROYAL PRINCESS
112 Chang Khlan Road
Tel: 281033/034; Fax: 281044
198 rooms. Centrally located and very popular with locals and visitors alike. Known for its high quality Chinese and Japanese restaurants. $$$$

WESTIN CHIANG MAI
324/11 Chiang Mai-Lamphun Road
Tel: 275300; Fax: 275299
526 rooms. Chiang Mai's biggest and most modern hotel. Scenic location on the banks of the Ping River. $$$$

AMARI RINCOME
1 Nimmanhamin Road
Tel: 221044; Fax: 221915
148 rooms. One of the oldest and best known in Chiang Mai. Its restaurants are known for their tasty buffets. $$$

CHIANG INN
100 Chang Khlan Road
Tel: 270070/071; Fax: 274299
170 rooms. Centrally located next to the night market, ideal downtown location. Good for shopping and nightlife. $$$

DIAMOND RIVERSIDE
33/10 Charoen Prathet Road
Tel: 270299, 270080; Fax: 271482.
300 rooms. Located on the banks of the Ping River with a top quality restaurant in Chiang Mai's oldest teak house. $$$

PORNPING
46-48 Chareon Prathet Road
Tel: 270099; Fax: 270119
325 rooms. Close to the banks of the Ping River, with great views from the upper floors. Home of the very popular Bubble Disco. $$$

QUALITY CHIANGMAI HILLS
18 Huai Kaeo Road
Tel: 210030/34; Fax: 210035
249 rooms. Located out of town near the lower slopes of Doi Suthep and Chiang Mai University. Several good restaurants in the vicinity. $$$

RIVER VIEW LODGE
25 Charoen Prathet Road, Soi 2
Tel: 271110; Fax: 279019
36 rooms. Right on the banks of the Ping River, a traditional place offering tranquillity in the heart of town and good Thai cuisine. $$$

SURIWONGZE ZENITH
110 Chang Khlan Road
Tel: 270051; Fax: 270063
168 rooms. Central downtown location close to the Night Market. Noted for its high quality yet reasonably priced Northern Thai restaurant. $$$

THE EMPRESS
199 Chang Khlan Road
Tel: 270240. Fax: 272467
375 rooms. Centrally located hotel with a good Chinese restaurant. $$$

GALARE
7/1 Charoen Prathet Road
Tel: 273885; Fax: 279088
35-room guesthouse. Conveniently located for the night market right next to the Galare Food Centre. $$

TOP NORTH
15 Moonmuang Road Soi 2
Tel: 278684; Fax: 278485
90-room guesthouse with swimming pool. Well placed for the historic Old City and Thapae Gate areas. $$

DARET'S HOUSE
4/5 Chaiyaphum Road
Tel: 235440
20-room guesthouse. A favourite with the back-packers, complete with a good restaurant. $

Eco-friendly travel

JE T'AIME
247-9 Charoen Rat Road
Tel: 241942
24-room guesthouse. Pleasantly located on the east bank of the Ping River. $

Mae Rim

ERAWAN RESORT
30 Moo 2
Tel: 297078
59 rooms. Charming cottages in an extensive park built by a lake. Beautiful mountain views. $$$

THE REGENT CHIANG MAI
502 Moo 1 Mae Rim-Samoeng Road
Tel: 2298181; Fax: 298189
True to the Regent name, these are the most luxurious accommodations found in North Thailand. The 'Modern Lanna' pavilion-style rooms are set amidst rice fields which are still worked. $$$$

MAE SA RESORT
KM 3 Mae Rim-Samoeng Road
Individual bungalows with full facilities and access to a 9-hole golf course. $$

MAE SA VALLEY
86 Mu 2, Mae Sa
Tel: 297980
Well appointed bungalows and restaurant amidst a very attractive setting of tropical flowers and trees. $$

Chiang Dao

CHIANG DAO HILLS RESORT
KM 100 Chiang Mai-Fang Highway
Tel: 236995; Fax: 251372

Attractive tourist bungalows in a pristine setting; probably the best place to stay between Chiang Mai and Thaton. Restaurant serving Thai and Western dishes. $$

PIANGDAO
Soi 1, Main Highway
10-room guesthouse. Basic, Chinese-style wooden hotel. No outstanding features, but cheap and well located for exploring Chiang Dao caves. $

Chiang Rai

DUSIT ISLAND RESORT
1129 Kraisorasit Road
Tel: 715777; Fax: 715801
288 rooms. Situated by the banks of the Kok River, ideal for long-tail boat trips upriver to Thaton. $$

WIANG INN
893 Phaholyothin Road
Tel: 711543; Fax: 711877
260 rooms. Very comfortable rooms at reasonable prices. Facilities include a swimming pool, bar, restaurant, coffee shop and disco. $$

WANG COME
869/90 Prem Wipak Road
Tel: 711800; Fax: 712973
221 rooms. Comfortable rooms but it may be necessary to bargain; some visitors have reported a two-tier pricing system for Thais and non-Thais. Facilities include a disco, coffeeshop and nightclub. $$

GOLDEN TRIANGLE G.H.
590 Phaholyothin Road
Tel: 711339; Fax: 713963
9-room guesthouse. Popular and deservedly so. Stylish rooms, a Japanese-style garden, plus an in-house travel agency. $$

MAE KOK VILLA
445 Singhalai Road
Tel: 711786
44-room guesthouse. Friendly, clean, and homely place with comfortable rooms. $

Fang

CHOKE THANI HOTEL
425 Mu 5 Chotana
Tel: 451252

60 rooms. Top hotel here (this is not a claim to luxury). For an overnight in Fang, it's comfortable and convenient. $$

Tha Ton

MAEKOK RIVER LODGE
On the Kok River, near the bridge
Tel: 215366; Fax: 459329
The best place to stay – and to eat – not only in Tha Ton, but in the Fang area. The interesting 'Track of the Tiger' tours are organised for visitors free of charge. $$

THIP'S TRAVELLERS HOUSE
Next to the bridge over the Kok River
Tel: 245538.
Simple guesthouse in a beautiful location right on the banks of the Kok River. $

Mae Sai

WANG THONG
299 Phaholyothin Road
Tel: 731248; Fax: 731249
New hotel catering to visiting businessmen. Has pool and restaurants. $$

MAE SAI
125/5 Phaholyothin Road
Tel: 731462
50 rooms. Centrally located on the main road leading to the bridge to Burma. Adequate, clean and comfortable. $

Sop Ruak

THE GOLDEN TRIANGLE HOTEL
222 Golden Triangle, Sop Ruak
Tel: 784001/5; Fax: 784006
An attractive resort offering well-appointed rooms with great views over the Mekong to Burma and Laos. $$$

LE MERIDIEN BAAN BORAN
Golden Triangle, Sop Ruak
Tel: 784078; Fax: 784090
Luxurious Thai-style resort with fine views and good restaurants. $$$

Chiang Saen

JIM'S GUEST HOUSE
Golden Triangle Road
Small and quiet establishment with a pleasant atmosphere by the banks of the Mekong River. $$

CHIANG SAEN G.H.
45 Tambon Wiang
18 rooms. Reasonably priced, basic, clean and close to the Mekhong. $

Mae Hong Son

HOLIDAY INN MAE HONG SON
Khunlum Prapas Road
Tel: 612212; Fax: 611524
114 rooms. First class hotel with splendid mountain views. Facilities include pool, disco and restaurants. $$$

TARA MAE HONG SON
149 Mu 8 Tambol Pang Mu
Tel: 611483; Fax: 611252
104 rooms. Without doubt the best accommodation in Mae Hong Son. $$$

Lush gardens surround most hotels

PIYA GUEST HOUSE
1 Soi 3, Khunlum Prapas Road
Tel: 611260
A good guest house right on the lake. If you stay here don't forget to rise at dawn and watch the morning mist floating above the nearby waters. $

Pai

RIM PAI COTTAGES
17 Moo 3, Wiang Tai
Tel: 699133
Individual cottages by the river. The room rates include breakfast. $$

CHARLIE'S HOUSE
5, Rungsiyanon Road
Tel: 699039
Perhaps the friendliest and best appointed guesthouse in town, Charlie's is often full in the high season (November to January), so it is advisable to book ahead. $

Mae Sariang

MIT AREE HOTEL
Mae Sariang Road
Tel: 681109.
67 rooms. The only hotel in Mae Sariang, though there are a number of guest houses. Nothing to write home about, but adequate rooms at reasonable prices. Located conveniently close to the bus station. $

HEALTH AND EMERGENCIES

Hygiene

Drink bottled water or soft drinks and save tap water for bathing and teeth-brushing. Most hotels and large restaurants offer bottled water and clean ice. Mineral water is both cheap and easily available from roadside stalls or supermarkets. Thai chefs understand the importance of hygiene and the chances of becoming ill from food poisoning is minimal.

With its thriving nightlife and transient population, Thailand is a magnet for venereal disease. AIDS is on the rise, so there is even more reason to be careful. Condoms are sold everywhere.

Pharmaceuticals are produced to international standards and pharmacies are required to have registered pharmacists on the premises. Most pharmacy personnel in the shopping and business areas speak some English.

Health Precautions

Malaria has not been eradicated in the hills of the North and the occasional case still surfaces, especially during the rainy season. In most major populated areas, you will not have a problem.

Do not put your faith completely in anti-malarial pills as they do not protect against the several new strains of malaria. Your best advice is to avoid being bitten by using plenty of insect repellent and a mosquito net while you sleep.

Avoid wearing dark-coloured clothes as they tend to attract mosquitoes. See a doctor and do not accept flu as a diagnosis if you develop a fever after you return from a trek. Insist on a blood test and mention the possibility you may have contracted malaria.

The incidence of rabies is not high, but you should still take immediate action if you are bitten by a dog: Wipe off the saliva from the wounds and wash thoroughly under a running tap or with plenty of water for at least five minutes, using soap or detergent. Apply an antiseptic (but do not use cetrimide).

Note the features of the dog and the particulars of its owner, if any. If it has an owner or can be kept under restraint, ask somebody to keep it under observation for the next 10 days. If the dog is still alive after 10 days, it is not rabid. But if it dies, it should be taken to a hospital laboratory to determine whether it died of rabies or some other cause.

Immediately after being bitten, consult a doctor and insist on starting the full course of six injections immediately. This is crucial if the bite is on the head or neck, especially for children.

The injections should be administered on the day of the being bitten, and on days 3, 7, 14, 30 and 90 after that. If the dog is still alive on the 10th day after the bite, the last three injections may be remitted.

Hospitals

Chiang Mai

LANNA HOSPITAL
Off the Superhighway on the northeast side of town
Tel: 211037/41

CHIANGMAI RAM HOSPITAL
8/4 Boon Ruangrit Road
(near Sri Tokyo Hotel)
Tel: 224851

Chiang Rai

CHIANG RAI PRACHURUKHRO HOSPITAL
Sathanpayaban Road
Tel: 711300

Lamphun

LAMPHUN HOSPITAL
Chamathewi Road
Tel: 511034

โรงพยาบาลปาย
PAI HOSPITAL

Mae Hong Son

SRISONGWAN HOSPITAL
Singharat Bamrung Road
Tel: 611378

Clinics

Chiang Mai

LOI KROA CLINIC
62/2 Loi Kroh Road
Tel: 271571

CHARD CHAI CLINIC
252/5-6 Phra Pokklao Road
Tel: 218181-2

Chiang Rai

CHIANG RAI CLINIC
234 Thanalai Road
Tel: 711234

Crime

A special Tourist Police force assists travellers with inquiries or recovery of stolen goods. It is at the ground floor of the Tourism Authority of Thailand office on the Chiang Mai-Lamphun Road. Tel: 248974. A new Tourist Police number, 1699, can be dialled from anywhere within the country.

There have been cases of unauthorised use of credit cards left in the safety deposit boxes of some of the guesthouses. It is probably best if you leave home without it; if it is stolen in the hills you will not be able to inform the card company until you get back to Chiang Mai.

In general, exercise caution when using credit cards. If someone has to take the card elsewhere to check your credit line, go with him.The incidence of armed robberies involving trekkers has declined but there are still occasional problems. The perpetrators are usually hilltribesmen and, quite often, employees of rival trekking companies trying to discredit popular firms. Carry what you need and no more.

COMMUNICATIONS & NEWS

Postal Services

The General Post Office (tel: 241070) is at Charoen Muang Road, near the railway station). Post offices are open Monday to Friday, 8.30am to 4.30pm. There are a number of sub-post offices in town, a useful one is on Praisani Road on the north side of Tha Phae Road, before reaching Nawarat Bridge. The post office at the airport is open daily from 8.30am to 8pm.

The Tourism Authority of Thailand (TAT) in Chiang Mai offers a mail and message service so that friends can send you letters. Get them to address the letters to you, care of: The Tourism Authority of Thailand, 105/1 Chiang Mai-Lamphun Road, Chiang Mai 50000, Thailand.

Telephones

Large hotels provide long-distance telephone and fax services. There is also a long-distance service at the General Post Office and at private shops along Chang Khlan and other streets in Chiang Mai. Some booths charge a base three minutes for overseas calls. Fax services are also available on request.

To call anywhere in Chiang Mai and the North from overseas, dial the Thailand country code 66, this is followed by the prefix 53.

When calling Chiang Mai and the North from elsewhere in Thailand, use the prefix 053 only.

To call overseas directly, you first dial the international access code 001; this is followed by the country code: For example: Australia (61); France (33); Germany

(49); Italy (39); Japan (81); Netherlands (31); Spain (34); UK (44); for USA and Canada (1).

If using US credit phone card, dial the company's access number:
Sprint tel: 001 99913 877
AT&T tel: 001 999 1 1111
MCI tel: 001 999 1 2001

Shipping

The big shops will generally handle shipping for you but if you have bought items at a number of shops and want to ship them yourself, go to the General Post Office which sells special cardboard shipping cartons. If you have a big shipment, utilise the services of these shipping companies:

CHIANG MAI AIR CARGO
234/2 Wua Lai Road
Tel: 274705

HONG KONG INTERNATIONAL MOVERS
13/7-8 Moo 1, Sankampaeng Road
Tel: 246951

Media

Thailand's English daily newspapers, the *Bangkok Post* and the *Nation* are available in Chiang Mai before 11am each day. Both these newspapers are morning papers. Hotels and shops also offer British, German and French newspapers but they are expensive.

Chiang Mai University broadcasts news and cultural programs in English daily between 6–8.30am and 6–10pm on 96.5 MHz FM. Light music is also broadcast daily on 100.8 MHz FM.

USEFUL INFORMATION

Maps

A Pocket Guide for Motorcycle Touring in North Thailand by David Unkovich is a guidebook rather than a map, but it is an accurate survey of the roads and touring conditions in North Thailand. It contains 23 strip maps, and is simple to use.

Like her popular *Bangkok Market Map*, Nancy Chandler's colourful *Chiang Mai Market Map* is a detailed guide to the bargain shopping spots of the city and a mine of minutiae that make shopping fun.

Bookshops

SURIWONG BOOK CENTRE
54/1-5 Sri Dornchai Road
Tel: 2810525

D.K. BOOK HOUSE
79/1 Kotchasarn Road
Tel: 207556

Possibly the best collection of books, magazines, newspapers, guide books and maps in Chiang Mai.

Export Permits

The Fine Arts Department prohibits the export of all Buddha images and that of other deities, and fragments (hands or heads) of images dating from before the 18th century. If you purchase one, the shop can register it for you. Otherwise, you must take it to the Fine Arts Department in Bangkok on Na Prathat Road across from Sanam Luang, together with two postcard-sized photos of it. Export fees range from 50 to 200 baht, depending on the antiquity of the piece.

Fake antiques do not require export permits but Thai Airport Customs officials are not art experts and may mistake it for a genuine piece. If it looks authentic, clear it at the Fine Arts Department to avoid problems later.

SPORTS

Fitness Parks

Chiang Mai has two fitness parks. **Huai Kaeo Fitness Park** is the older and more attractive of the two. It is wedged between the Arboretum and the Zoo on Huai Kaeo Road. The other is on the Suthep end of Nimmanhamin Road. Both are open from 5am–10pm.

Hash House Harriers

The Harriers were founded by British soldiers in Malaysia as a means of making running fun. The 'Hares' string a paper trail through the back-country, laying down as many false clues as they do true ones. The 'Hounds' follow the trail through marshes, canals and rice fields to reach the goal: frosty bottles of beer. The Hash meets every Saturday. Call Jad at 818109 or David at 278503 for details.

Horse Riding

Lanna Horse Riding Club: Located near the race course on Mae Rim Road, the club charges riding fees by the hour. Saddles are provided, and helmets can be hired. Tel: 221911.

Tennis

If the **Amari Rincome Hotel** courts are not used by guests, they can be rented by outsiders. Otherwise, go to **Anantasiri Court**, 90/1 Superhighway (opposite Chiang Mai Museum). Tel: 222210. Daily 7am–7pm except Tuesdays. You can rent tennis rackets, balls and hire an instructor for coaching sessions here.

Windsurfing

Lake windsurfing is available at Huai Tung Tao, **Agricultural Development Centre** (Chotana Road, enroute to Mae Rim).

Golf

Lanna Golf Course: Chotana Road (tel: 221911). An 18-hole course. Daily 6am–6pm.
Gymkhana Club Golf Course: Rat Uthit Road off the Chiang Mai-Lamphun Road (tel: 247352). A nine-hole course on the grounds of the city's oldest private club.
Green Valley Golf Club: An 18-hole course located on the right-hand side on reaching the district town of Mae Rim (tel: 297426).
Chiang Mai Golf Driving Range: 239/3 Wua Lai Road (tel: 201606). Open 7am–10pm.

LANGUAGE

Origins and Intonation

For centuries, the Thai language, rather than tripping from foreigners' tongues, has been tripping them up. Its roots go back to the place Thais originated from, in the hills of southern Asia but overlaid by Indian influences. From the original settlers come the five tones which seem designed to frustrate visitors — one sound with five different tones to mean five different things.

When you mispronounce, you don't simply say a word incorrectly, you say another word entirely. It is not unusual to see a semi-fluent foreigner standing before a Thai running through the scale of tones until suddenly a light of recognition dawns on his companion's face. There are misinformed visitors who will tell you that tones are not important. These people do not communicate with Thais; they communicate at them in a one-sided exchange that frustrates both parties.

Thai Names

From the languages of India have come polysyllabic names and words. Thai names are among the longest in the world. Every Thai first and surname has a meaning. Thus by learning the meaning of the name of everyone you meet, you would acquire quite an extensive vocabulary.

There is no universal transliteration system from Thai into English, which is why names and street names can be spelled three different ways. For example, the surname Chumsai is written Chumsai, Jumsai and Xoomsai depending on the family. This confuses even the Thais. If you ask a Thai how you spell something, he may well reply 'how do you want to spell it?' Likewise, Bangkok's thoroughfare of

Ratchadamnern is also spelt as Rajdamnern. The spellings will differ from map to map, and book to book.

Phonology

The way Thai consonants are written in English often confuses foreigners. An 'h' following a letter like 'p', and 't' gives the letter a soft sound; without the 'h' the sound is more explosive. Thus, 'ph' is not pronounced 'f' but as a soft 'p'. Without the 'h', the 'p' has the sound of a very hard 'b'. The word Thanon (street) is pronounced 'tanon' in the same way as 'Thailand' is not meant to sound like 'Thighland.' Similarly, final letters are often not pronounced as they look. A 'j' on the end of a word is pronounced 't'; 'l' is pronounced as an 'n'. To complicate matters further, many words end with 'se' or 'r' which are not pronounced.

Vowels are pronounced like this: 'i' as in sip, 'ii' as in seep, 'e' as in bet, 'a' as in pun, 'aa' as in pal, 'u' as in pool, 'o' as in so, 'ai' as in pie, 'ow' as in cow, 'aw' as in paw, 'iw' as in you, 'oy' as in toy.

In Thai, the pronoun 'I' and 'me' use the same word but it is different for males and females. Men use the word *phom* when referring to themselves; women say *chan* or *diichan*. Men use *khrap* at the end of a sentence when addressing either a male or a female i.e. pai (f) *nai, khrap* (h) (where are you going? sir). Women add the word *kha* to their statements as in *pai* (f) *nai, kha* (h).

To ask a question, add a high tone *mai* to the end of the phrase i.e. *rao pai* (we go) or *rao pai mai* (h) (shall we go?). To negate a statement, insert a falling tone mai between the subject and the verb i.e. *rao pai* (we go), *rao mai pai* (we don't go). 'Very' or 'much' are indicated by adding *maak* to the end of a phrase i.e. *ron* (hot), *ron maak* (very hot).

Listed below is a small but helpful vocabulary list. The five tones have been indicated by appending letters after them ie high (h), low (l), middle (m), rising (like asking a question) (r), and falling (like suddenly understanding something as in 'ohh, I see') (f). Note: Thais living in the seven Northern provinces speak a language amongst themselves known as *kham muang*, or the language of the country. This is quite different from Bangkok Thai. These days, though, nearly everyone speaks Bangkok Thai and casual visitors trying out their language skills will have enough on their hands with the phrases shown below.

Useful Phrases

Numbers
1/Nung (m)
2/Song (r)
3/Sam (r)
4/Sii (m)
5/Haa (f)
6/Hok (m)
7/Jet (m)
8/Pat (m)
9/Kow (f)
10/Sip (m)
11/Sip Et (m, m)
12/Sip Song (m, r)
13/Sip Sam (m, r) and so on
20/Yii Sip (m, m)
30/Sam Sip (f, m) and so on
100/Nung Roi (m, m)
1,000/Nung Phan (m, m)
Days of the Week
Monday/Wan Jan
Tuesday/Wan Angkan
Wednesday/Wan Phoot
Thursday/Wan Pharuhat
Friday/Wan Sook
Saturday/Wan Sao
Sunday/Wan Athit
Today/Wan nii (h)
Yesterday/Mua wan nii (h)
Tomorrow/Prung nii (h)
When/Mua (f) rai

Greetings and others
Hello, goodbye
Sawasdee (a man then says khrup; a woman says kha; thus sawasdee khrup, or kha)
How are you?/Khun sabai dii, mai (h)
Well, thank you/Sabai dii, Khapkhun
Thank you very much/Khapkhun Maak
May I take a photo?
Thai roop (f) noi, dai (f) mai (h)
Never mind/Mai (f) pen rai
I cannot speak Thai
Phuut Thai mai (f) dai (f)
I can speak a little Thai

Phuut Thai dai (f) nit (h) diew
Where do you live?
Khun yoo thii (f) nai (r)
What is this called in Thai?
An nii (h), kaw riak aray phasa Thai
How much?/Thao (f) rai

Directions and Travel
Go/Pai
Come/Maa
Where/Thii (f) nai (r)
Right/Khwaa (r)
Left/Sai (h)
Turn/Leo
Straight ahead/Trong pai
Please slow down/Cha cha noi
Stop here/Yood thii (f) nii (f)
Fast/Raew
Hotel/Rong raam
Street/Thanon
Lane/Soi
Bridge/Saphan
Police Station/Sathanii Dtam Ruat

Other Handy Phrases
Yes/Chai (f)
No/Mai (f) chai (f)
Do you have...?/Mii...mai (h)
Expensive/Phaeng
Do you have something cheaper?
Mii arai thii thook (l) kwa, mai (h)
Can you lower the price a bit?
Kaw lot noi dai (f) mai (h)
Do you have another colour?
Mii sii uhn mai (h)
Too big/Yai kern pai
Too small/Lek kern pai
Do you have bigger?

Mii arai thii yai kwa mai (h)
Do you have smaller?
Mii arai thii lek kwa mai (h)
Hot (heat hot)/Ron (h)
Hot (spicy)/Phet
Cold/Yen
Sweet/Waan (r)
Sour/Prio (f)
Delicious/Aroy
I do not feel well/Mai (f) sabai

Glossary of Temple Terms

Bot or*bosot*, this is the ordination hall, usually open only to the monks. Some temples do not have a *bot*.
Chedi: Often interchangeable with stupa. Mound surmounted by a spire in which relics of the Buddha are supposedly kept. Influential families also build small chedis to hold the ashes of their forebears.
Chofah: The bird-like decoration on the end of a *bot* or *viharn* roof.
Galae: 'horns' at peak of a Lanna house.
Ku: A square, normally gilded, brick and stucco structure in the middle of a northern *viharn* that houses a Buddha image.
Naga: Serpent, usually running down the roof's edge sheltering meditating Buddha.
Prang: An Ayutthayan-style *chedi*, looking somewhat like a vertical ear of corn. Wat Arun is a main example.
Sala: An open-sided pavilion.
Viharn: The sermon hall, the busiest building in a wat. A temple may have more than one.
Wat: Translated as 'temple', but describing a collection of buildings and monuments within a compound wall.

Tourist Information

The Tourism Authority of Thailand (TAT) is the Thai government's official tourism promotion organization. The head office in Bangkok at 372 Bamrung Muang Road (tel: 226 0060, 226 0072, 226 0085) will provide you with essential tourist information. In Chiang Mai, the TAT is at 105/1 Chiang Mai-Lamphun Road (tel: 248604, 248607). Open daily from 8.30am–4.30pm). On the ground floor is the office of the Tourist Police (tel: 248974).

Travel magazines are offered free at hotel reception desks. Although advertiser-oriented, they provide up-to-date information on current events. The English-language *Welcome to Chiang Mai* is the most comprehensive. For Internet junkies, TAT's travel information web site is at http://www.cs.ait.ac.th/tat/. The TAT's e-mail address for sending inquiries is tat@cs.ait.ac.th.

Banks

Chiang Mai

BANGKOK BANK
53-9 Tha Phae Road
Tel: 270121

BANK OF ASIA
149/1-3 Chang Khlan Road
Tel: 282903

SIAM COMMERCIAL BANK
17 Tha Phae Road
Tel: 276122

THAI FARMERS BANK
169-71 Tha Phae Road
Tel: 270151

Chiang Rai

BANGKOK BANK
517 Suksathit Road
Tel: 711248

SIAM COMMERCIAL BANK
552 Tanalai Road
Tel: 711515

THAI FARMERS BANK
537 Bupprakarn Road
Tel: 711515

Mae Hong Son

BANGKOK BANK
68 Khunlum Prapas Road
Tel: 611546

THAI FARMERS BANK
76 Khunlum Prapas Road
Tel: 611556

Airline Offices

Chiang Mai

AIR MANDALAY
92/3 Sridonchai Road
Tel: 818049

LAO AVIATION
240 Phra Pokklao Road
Tel: 418258

MALAYSIA AIRLINES
153 Sri Dornchai Road
Tel: 276523

ORIENT EXPRESS AIR
Suriwongse Zenith Hotel
110 Chang Khlan Road
Tel: 818092

SILK AIR
Mae Ping Hotel
153 Sri Dornchai Road
Tel: 276496

THAI INTERNATIONAL
240 Phra Pokklao Road
Tel: 210043, 211044
Airport: 270222

Chiang Rai

THAI INTERNATIONAL
870 Phaholyothin Road
Tel: 711179, 713863
Airport: 711464

Mae Hong Son

THAI INTERNATIONAL
71 Singhanathamrung Road
Tel: 611297, 611194
Airport: 611367

FURTHER READING

History

An Asian Arcady, Reginald Le May. White Lotus, Bangkok. 1986. An excellent account of the history of the North.

The Politics of Heroin in Southeast Asia, Alfred W. McCoy. Harper and Row, New York. 1989. A compulsively detailed study of the heroin trade in the region but particularly in the Golden Triangle.

Lanna Textiles, Patricia Cheesman and Songsak Prangwatthanakun. Suriwong Book Centre, Chiang Mai. 1987. A superb study of many of the woven fabrics found in Lanna.

A Life Apart, Jon Boyes and S. Piraban. Suriwong Book Centre, Chiang Mai. 1989. A series of 23 fascinating interviews with members of six hilltribes about their lives, customs and perceptions.

A Trekkers Guide to the Hilltribes of Northern Thailand, John R. Davies. Footloose Books, Wiltshire, U.K. 1989. Good overview of hilltribes and their customs.

Insight Guide: Thailand and *Insight Pocket Guide: Thailand*, Apa Publications. Both have sections on Chiang Mai and also on northern Thailand.

Consul in Paradise, W.A.R. Wood. Souvenir Press, London. First published in 1965. Reprinted in 1991. The memoirs of a cheerful Englishman who arrived in Chiang Mai as a translator in 1908 and ultimately became the British Consul.

Teak-Wallah, Reginald Campbell. Oxford University Press, Singapore. 1986. The memoirs of an Englishman working in Thailand's forests in the 1920s.

Essays on Thai Folklore, Rajadhon, Phya Anuman. Bangkok: DK Books. A description of Thai ceremonies, festivals and rites of passage.

The Arts of Thailand, Van Beek, Steve & Tettoni L.I. London, Thames & Hudson, 1991. Lavishly illustrated.

Wat Chiang Mun, built by the founder of Chiang Mai

Index

ACKNOWLEDGMENTS

Photography	Steve van Beek *and*
93	Dallas and John Heaton
18, 20, 33, 34, 39, 41, 44, 50, 55, 80, 83	
94, 95, 98, 105, 106, 107, 114	Ingo Jezierski
92	Jean-Leo Dugast
Front cover, 6, 7, 10, 11, 65, 69, 85	Luca Invernizzi Tettoni
32, 39	Marcus Wilson Smith
55	Oliver Hargreave/CPA
Back cover	Steve Van Beek
Update Editor	David Henley
Maps	Berndtson & Berndtson
Cover Design	Klaus Geisler